D1535427

Search for Nothing

Richard P. Hardy

�֍ SEARCH FOR NOTHING

THE LIFE OF JOHN OF THE CROSS

Crossroad · New York

Acknowledgments

Excerpts from *The Collected Works of St. John of the Cross*, translated by
Kieran Kavanaugh and Otilio Rodriguez. Copyright © 1964 by Washing-
ton Province of Discalced Carmelites, Inc., ICS Publications, 2131 Lincoln
Road, N.E., Washington, D.C. 20002.

Excerpts from *The Complete Works of St. Teresa*, translated and edited by
E. Allison Peers. London: Sheed and Ward, 1972.

1982

The Crossroad Publishing Company
575 Lexington Avenue, New York, NY 10022

Printed in the United States of America

Library of Congress Cataloging in Publication Data

Hardy, Richard P.
Search for nothing.

Bibliography: p. 147
1. John of the Cross, Saint, 1542–1591.
2. Christian saints — Spain — Biography.
3. Mysticism — Spain. 4. Mysticism — 1450–1800.
I. Title.
BX4700.J7H37 1982   271'.73'024 [B] 82-13081
ISBN 0-8245-0499-2

Well and good if all things change,
Lord God, provided we are rooted in You.

Sayings of Light and Love, no. 30

To my son Sophâl,
whose Kampuchean homeland
lived years in a dark night
(1975–1979) that forced
thousands like him to flee.

Contents

Introduction   1

 I. Juan de Yepes, The Young Man   5
    (1542-1564)

 II. The Young Carmelite and the Reform   21
    (1564-1572)

III. Avila and The Monastery of the Encarnacion   43
    (1572-1577)

IV. The Dark Night of Imprisonment in Toledo   61
    (1577-1578)

 V. Fray Juan de la Cruz' Leadership in Andalusia   79
    (1578-1588)

VI. The Final Years, Segovia and Ubeda   99
    (1588-1591)

    Epilogue   113

    Selected Texts from the Works
      of Fray Juan de la Cruz   131

    For Further Reading   147

Introduction

Since I began studying the work of Fray Juan de la Cruz some fifteen years ago, I have been ill at ease with most of the biographies written about him. Though I was impressed by Jean Baruzi's biographical section in his classic work, *Saint Jean de la Croix et le problème de l'expérience mystique*,[1] other works in the same vein did not quite reach this stature. Even the scholarly work by Crisogono de Jesús and that by Bruno de Jésus-Marie,[2] as well as the more popular ones published in the last century or early part of this century did not seem to really apprehend Fray Juan de la Cruz the man. Although these authors had worked with the manuscripts and had attempted to be faithful to the witnesses of his time, they continued a tradition of hagiography. In fact, they created a saint in their own image of what sanctity meant for them.

Each age creates from its own culture and experience. Thus these biographers of Fray Juan portrayed a dismal, dark personality who seemed bent upon escaping this world and entering the next. Their Juan de la Cruz was seen as a paragon of virtue and strength. According to them, miracles and heavenly hosts always protected him from evil. The authors seemed to delight in vying with each other in presenting some atrocious practices in which Fray Juan was supposed to have engaged in the name of asceticism and mysticism. The result is a view of someone who seems hardly human. As presented by them, he was not one who could be imitated in the twentieth century. Nor do they inspire much desire to imitate such a person. However, despite all of this, even these authors and the witnesses they seem to depend upon could not help seeing in Fray Juan some very human qualities: his sense of humor, his love for his family, his deep love of beauty, concern for his neighbor, and love of delightful things. But these were not seen as the stuff of a saint — either by his previous biographers or by his contemporaries. Consequently, these characteristics were either forgotten or hidden among the rest, remaining lost in what was considered in sixteenth-century Spain to be the life of a true saint.

For me these biographies did not reveal the true Fray Juan de la Cruz, the man I had come to know in reading his *Spiritual Canticle* or his *Living Flame of Love*. They did not adequately reflect the author of the sensual, world-loving *Romances on Creation*. They did not really help me to understand his counsels to religious about detachment. Nor did they help me to penetrate the meaning of his *Ascent of Mount Carmel* or *The Dark Night of the Soul*. After reading these works and biographies, I would ask myself, "Was Fray Juan indeed such a paradox? Am I to admit that his life and his works simply were too disparate and should always be kept apart?" Somehow I could not answer yes to these questions.

The more that I read and reread his works, the more I found that they spoke of a different man, different from the one I had read about in the biographies. So, I set out to do something about it. I determined to research his life once more. I went to Rome and worked in the Vatican Secret Archives, which hold some of the canonization and beatification documents, invaluable sources for the biographer of Fray Juan. In the same city, I was able to work in the library of the Teresianum, which has some of the earliest biographies of Fray Juan. Here Padre Eulogio Pacho, ocd and his team of Discalced Carmelite researchers and scholars helped me greatly. They introduced me to the Calced Carmelites, who also let me use their library facilities. I then travelled throughout Spain, seeing the places Fray Juan himself had seen and lived in, as well as working on early documents which were to be found in the Discalced Carmelite monastery in Ubeda, where Fray Juan had died, and in the Biblioteca Nacional de Madrid, whose staff was most eager to assist me.

Slowly a new figure emerged: a man, a human being who had fallen in love with God IN the world. I discovered a man who is indeed a saint, but not because he fled the world. I found a man who had discovered in his life that sanctity meant searching for and finding God in THIS world of ours. Here was a man for whom the incarnation of the Word of God in Jesus meant the consecration of the world and its history. For Fray Juan, God was one who speaks in time, in life, in the world.

What I have tried to do in this short book is to present this man, Fray Juan de la Cruz (1542-1591) as I have come to see him. I have written it for anyone who is interested in coming to know him as a human being who became through and in his life a man of God, a saint. I have written it to help those who would like to read his writings and understand them more clearly.

My sources for this work have been the earliest manuscripts that relate what witnesses had to say about him, as well as the first biographies and the works of Fray Juan himself. The dialogues found herein have been constructed from material found in the manuscripts. Those that are direct quotations have their respective footnotes giving the proper reference. Finally, in the appendix of the book I have listed the main biographies of Fray Juan de la Cruz and a selection of texts from his own works. The latter is for those who would like to see what this new interpretation of his life can mean as one tries to read his works. I hope this study will release some new insights into the authentic Fray Juan and his approach to the Christian mystical life.

Many people have been involved in helping me to bring this book to completion. I would thank them all and in particular my special thanks to: Dr. Kenneth Russell, researcher, St. Paul University, who had the great patience and kindness to read the manuscript and offer many pertinent suggestions for improvement; Padre Eulogio Pacho, ocd and the staff of the Teresianum and the library for their help; my colleagues in the Faculty of Theology of Saint Paul University, Ottawa, Ontario, Canada, who encouraged me in the research and writing, and Mr. Paul Poirier, Administrative Assistant to the Dean, and especially the secretaries, Mss. Danielle Chartrand and Vivianne Robidoux, who bravely took on the task of deciphering my script to type the manuscript. I would like as well to express my gratitude to the Social Sciences and Humanities Research Council of Canada for the leave fellowship grant they awarded me to finish the research for this book.

NOTES

1. Jean Baruzi, *Saint Jean de la Croix et le problème de l'expérience mystique* (Paris: Librarie Félix Alcan, 1924).

2. Crisogono de Jesús, ocd, *Vida y Obras de San Juan de la Cruz* (Textual revisions and critical notes by Matías del Niño Jesús, ocd and critical edition of the works by Lucinio del SS. Sacramento, ocd), (Madrid: Biblioteca de Autores Cristianos, 1964). (Hereafter this work is referred to as BAC.) This life is certainly extremely well done and provides an excellent setting for Fray Juan de la Cruz. However, the author does not seem to have always judiciously selected the more reliable witnesses and documents upon which to base his story.

The other major biography in our century is that of Bruno de Jésus-Marie, *Saint Jean de la Croix* (Bruge: Desclée de Brouwer, 1961).

I

Juan de Yepes,
The Young Man (1542–1564)

The drama neared its completion. As the wintry winds blew through the narrow, cobblestoned streets and pathways of Ubeda in southern Spain, the monks in the Carmelite monastery gathered in silence. In a cramped room on the upper level lay an emaciated tiny friar—Fray Juan de la Cruz. The labored breathing of the frail monk told all that the end was near. While faint whispers of prayers faded into silence, the candles his fellow monks held in their hands cast eerie, moving shadows on the wall.

Suddenly the silence was shattered by the sound of the monastery bell. It called the friars to the recitation of morning prayer. As the familiar sound pierced his ears, Fray Juan opened his eyes and asked, "What was that bell for?" When told that it was the bell calling the brothers to the chapel for Matins, he relaxed on the pillow and smiled peacefully. They might be praying here, but he knew that he would be praying matins in Eternity. Shortly after midnight, on December 13–14, 1591, death came as another step in the life of Fray Juan de la Cruz. He died as he had lived, surrounded by those who liked him and those who did not. In the forty-nine years of his life, he had puzzled people. He had angered some; he had entertained others. But he loved them all. Each formed part of that search he had embarked upon so early in his youth.

Family and Youth

The sixteenth century was one of the most dynamic ones in the history of Spain. This land of rustic beauty achieved a greatness that would never again be equaled in her history. The famous couple Isabella and Ferdinand struggled and attained their goal of a united nation. Granada, freed from Moorish control in 1492, was yet to undergo the throes of the Inquisition, which struck fear in the hearts of so many Jews and followers of Islam. Nonetheless, it now became part of the Spanish nation once more.

The ports south of Granada on the Mediterranean bustled with activity. Dock workers loaded provisions for the New World colonies, while others unloaded galleons bulging with treasured cargo from those distant lands. Like a colony of ants, the workers streamed in endless lines hustling crates and boxes on and off the vessels. Those who had made the journey to the New World and lived to tell the tale entertained the crowds in the squares and taverns with stories of fantastic riches and high adventure.

At home Spain developed. Her art, music, and life became the envy of all. Her king was Emperor. Her influence extended to practically all of Europe and into the New World. Wealth abounded, at least for the nobles. But poverty oppressed the vast majority of the people. These two classes, the rich and poor, existed side by side—separated, however, by the invisible barriers of their respective worlds. As a rule people did not even attempt to bridge the chasm that kept them apart. Some, however, did dare to set conventions aside.

Gonzalo de Yepes and a woman called Catalina Alvarez were two such people. Gonzalo de Yepes came from an influential family in the region of Toledo in central Spain. For years their family members had been clerics or *mercaderes*. (Most were financiers whose large holdings enabled them to invest in manufacturing crafts and transportation.) This automatically made them a people of the upper class. Yet the family tree held secrets that it was best to keep hidden in that sensitive time. The Yepes family were *conversos,* that is, they were originally Jewish converts to Christianity.[1] To have had Jewish blood even several generations earlier made one suspect and hindered members of such a family from holding civil or ecclesiastical positions of power. The Inquisition kept such people under constant surveillance. Jealous citizens would often report them to the inquisitorial authorities who would strip them of their property, honor and position in the community. The Yepes hid their roots well.

Though the family was itself very wealthy, Gonzalo was not. Because he was an orphan, he lived with an uncle and his family. Eventually he worked for his uncle, which meant traveling a great deal, particularly in central and northern Spain.

It was in Fontiveros, a small town just north of Madrid, that Gonzalo, on a business trip to Medina del Campo on behalf of his uncle, met a young woman named Catalina Alvarez. Like Gonzalo, Catalina was originally from Toledo. A few years before Gonzalo entered her life, she was befriended by a widow from Fontiveros who offered to share her home with Catalina. Since her parents had both died, Catalina believed that she could start her life anew in this tiny village.

Gonzalo and Catalina fell in love. He could hardly wait to share his joy with his family. But when he announced his plans to marry they were horrified. They threatened to disown him and to number him among the dead if he went through with the proposed marriage. They knew Catalina was poor, but this was not the reason for their opposition. There was something much more serious in their eyes. Catalina's background, too, had its secrets. She was rumored to be either the daughter of a Moorish slave or of someone who had been burned at the stake for judaizing.[2] Marrying her might provoke an investigation that would uncover their own Jewish background. They regarded running such a risk as unthinkable. The more obdurate they became, the more Gonzalo and Catalina were determined to go ahead.

These two young stalwarts were unique indeed. Though gentle and loving, Gonzalo was principled and determined. His love was no infatuation that would fade as quickly as it had risen. A man who gave up a secure and comfortable life for an unknown future in marriage outside his class was one for whom love meant fidelity and sacrifice. Catalina herself was of the same mind.

Like her future husband she had been alone a good part of her life. For her, marrying Gonzalo did not mean a guarantee of comfort and social status. Love was the principal element in their relationship — an interesting fact in an age when most marriages were arranged and love was not a necessary ingredient. Convinced that their love for each other would sustain them, they married around the year 1529.

Though their life together was to be filled with moments of marvelous happiness, initially it was difficult. Gonzalo had to learn how to weave bonnets and thin veils for the ladies of the region. Weaving was not a trade in which one became wealthy, but it did provide the basic necessities for a family. The two of them worked together long and hard as they started their family.

By 1542, they had three sons. Francisco, the eldest, born around 1530, was to play an extremely important role in the life of his youngest brother, Juan (later Fray Juan de la Cruz) who was born in 1542.[3] The other son, Luis, was born sometime between the births of Francisco and Juan.

The family survived, but barely managed to maintain itself at the subsistence level. Food was often scarce. What little they had depended greatly upon their weaving skills, hard work, and the demand for their products. Their home became their factory. Colored threads, spools, and remnants littered the largest of the rooms, which they also used as a living and dining room. Colors and odors blended as did the sounds of the looms and shuttles moving along the unfolding cloth under the agile fingers of Catalina and Gonzalo. As he got older, Juan would help dress the looms. Even though he was the youngest, he had to bear his share of the work and responsibilities.

However, the strain of trying to earn enough for the family, the sadness he felt at being cut off from his relatives, and the lack of substantial food took their toll on Gonzalo. After fifteen or so years of this draining life, he fell ill. His illness dragged on for several years. His gradual decline meant that the members of the family felt even more pressed to pitch in to do their part to keep the family going.

Juan was deeply marked by his experience of caring for his ailing father during the two years of his decline. In later years, first as an adolescent and then as a Carmelite friar, Juan would demonstrate that this experience had taught him how to be gentle and considerate in the care of the sick. But this closeness to a dying father was not the only childhood experience that influenced him.

His father's inability to play a role in the family's "cottage industry" made it imperative that Juan learn more about weaving. His mother taught him a few things so that he could help her when she was busy caring for her dying husband. Juan remembered his weaving days when years later in one of his mystical poems he spoke of ". . . the veil of this sweet encounter."[4] The Spanish word translated as "veil" actually refers to the threads set into a weaver's loom. The natural events of work, life, and death made their imprint on the sensitive Juan de Yepes just as they do on every human being.

After two painful years of suffering, Juan's father died just before Juan turned eight years old. Catalina, left with three sons to care for, was desparate. What little money they had saved had been quickly used up during Gonzalo's illness. The remaining four members of the Yepes family suffered the consequences: destitution. Catalina gathered her courage and set off with her three sons to seek help from her husband's two brothers.

For Catalina, her children's well-being was first in her mind. Her hope, despite what she knew could be the outcome, was to have the brothers-in-law take care of at least one or perhaps two of her sons. She thought and questioned herself about this as she and her sons made their way slowly southward to Toledo. Their first stop after the wearying journey on foot was in the neighborhood of Torrijos, not far from Toledo, where one of Juan's uncles was Archdeacon. The uncle listened to his sister-in-law's plea, but responded negatively. He could not take them because they were too young. There was more to it than that and Catalina knew it. She was crushed. The division in the Yepes family caused by her marriage to Gonzalo so many years ago had not been mended. The passing of the years and the death of Gonzalo had done nothing to calm the waters, at least in this particular person. As Catalina and her little troop made their way to Galvez (about fifteen miles from Toledo) to make another appeal, she wondered if the reception would be the same as they had just experienced.

But things were very different in Galvez. Gonzalo's brother was a doctor. Like the youngest of her own children, he was called Juan de Yepes. He showed a real interest in Catalina and her family. Since he and his wife had no children of their own, the idea of having a son appealed to him. So he offered to take care of the oldest of her children, Francisco, who by now was a teenager. This relieved Catalina greatly for she saw that her eldest son now had a chance for a better life than what she could ever offer him. After staying a few days with her brother-in-law, she returned to Fontiveros with her two other sons, leaving Francisco in the doctor's care. However, things were not to be as ideal as she originally had thought.

Back at home, Catalina continued her work, but wondered how Francisco was doing in his new home. After several months had passed without any news from him, she decided to go back to see for herself how things were going. What she discovered shocked her. While the doctor had been extremely kind, his wife had not been. She had made Francisco work hard, kept him from going to school and showed him no love whatever. Upon discovering Francisco's predicament, Catalina took him back with her despite the doctor's vow that things would be different.

But in Fontiveros, things went from bad to worse. Catalina's weaving brought in little money. Moreover, Francisco, whose adolescence was well underway, seemed to be getting out of hand. He stayed out late and sometimes did not even come home at all. Catalina worried about him a great deal.[5] Then tragedy struck again. Luis, the middle brother, died.

Another move seemed to be the only way to survive. Yet Catalina was reluctant to leave because Fontiveros held so many memories for her. She had met her husband there; her children had been born there; it was her home. But it was clear that she had to leave. So, they went to Arevalo (not very far from Fontiveros) where she and Francisco continued to work as weavers. Things were better but still not good enough. So, shortly afterwards (around 1550-1551) they moved to Medina del Campo.

Medina del Campo was a bustling city situated just northwest of Madrid on the main road leading from Salamanca to Valladolid. Trade fairs were held there twice a year, during May and October. People from far-flung countries came there to participate in this biannual event. The merchants and financiers bartered goods from the East, spices and silks, books from distant countries, cloth, and exotic things from the New World. With them they also brought tales and news from far-off lands. During this time of festival the city was filled with excitement as traders told of happenings in their countries of origin. Once one fair was finished, preparations began immediately for the next one. Juan grew up in this atmosphere of excitement and activity. At a time when news spread mainly through domestic and foreign visitors, Juan was in closer contact with what was occurring in different parts of the world than most Spaniards.

The importance of this period in Juan's life is not to be belittled. By the time his family arrived in Medina del Campo, Juan was nine years old, an age when he would be impressed by new things. What he heard about the New World and what he saw in these annual trade fairs formed the young boy. He learned to listen and was continually discovering new and tantalizing things about the world far beyond the walls of this city. In Medina del Campo he could visit the Americas through the stories of those who had been there. He could smell the spices of the East with the merchants who brought them to sell. He knew what was happening politically, religiously, and socially in the municipal world around him just through observation. The throbbing life of the city became a major influence upon him. Being submerged in it made him receptive to the new things he encountered and open to the deep values he would hold all his life. The city was his school. Yet his education was not limited to listening to those who bartered and traded goods in a medieval fair.

At this time there existed a school called the Colegio de la Doctrina in Medina del Campo. There with other children who were either orphans or from poor families, Juan learned to read and write. Here he had his first real taste of formal learning and it was more or less a success. His brother tells us that after his mother put him in this school, he learned to read and write in just a few days.[6] However, in professional matters, his teachers thought much less of his abilities. They tried to teach him a trade — carpentry, tailoring, wood carving, painting — but he seemed unable to do well in any of these despite his eagerness to learn something that would enable him to help his family. These failures were disheartening for this conscientious boy of eleven or twelve.

But his life continued in the same vein as that of any boy of his age and social class. He learned to serve Mass at the Convento de la Magdalena which was the home of the Augustinian nuns. He worked and played, but because of what had already happened in his life he impressed others as being more sensitive and thoughtful than other boys his age. As he walked the cobblestoned streets from his house to the Convento, he thought about his future, his mother and his work.

Though he was just another small boy among many others, Don Alonso Alvarez de Toledo, the administrator of the Hospital de Las Bubas in Medina, took a special interest in him. He was struck by the young fellow's maturity and decided to do something to help him.

Don Alvarez offered Juan a job as a male nurse in his hospital. He had been observing young Juan at the Convento for several weeks and realized that Juan's attitude and qualities were just what the hospital needed. So one day he asked the little boy if he would accept work at the hospital. Juan, who had painful memories of his failure to learn a trade at the doctrine school that he had attended, jumped at the chance of having a job which would help his mother a little. When he accepted the offer, Juan resolved that this would not be another failure.

When Juan began to work at the hospital of Nuestra Señora de la Concepción (commonly called Las Bubas), there were forty-five to fifty beds. Sometimes there were more, for some patients would bring in their own. All beds that were solid, wooden frames with straw mattresses and pillows stuffed with wool were in one great room with no separations of any type between them.[7] Doña Teresa Enrriquez, Duchess of Maqueda, had founded the Hospital de Las Bubas in 1480 to treat people afflicted with ulcers and contagious diseases. (This meant, in fact, those suffering from venereal diseases.) It was one of the very few specialized hospitals in Medina del Campo. Because it cared for the poor with contractable illnesses, the hospital was located at some distance from the center of the city. Moreover, the fairs attracted prostitutes and encouraged the poor to pick up a little easy money by offering carnal services. This meant that the hospital was filled all year long. The physical, psychological and social suffering of the patients impressed young Juan de Yepes in the adolescent, formative years during which he lived and worked there.

Juan immersed himself in his work at once. His first concern was the sick. Though some of them were in terrible condition, he did all he could for them. Their open wounds and the anger and rejection they often expressed did not keep him from fulfilling his function. He would hold the weaker ones up to feed or bathe them and change their bandages when necessary. Touching them would certainly have repelled many others but Juan was determined not to flinch. He wanted them to see that he was there to help them and he showed it by coming close to them. The dying ones found him at their side, encouraging and comforting them as much as possible. Those who had no friends or relatives to visit them became the ones Juan would spend extra time with. When they were overcome by sadness and loneliness, Juan tried to make them happy.

In fact, Juan entertained them by telling stories and singing songs.[8] He loved to make people laugh, to lift up their spirits with music. He met their needs with as much care as he could muster at any given time — even if some days he could do little because he, too, was human and needed to be encouraged himself. Yet, for him, hospital work was not simply a job. He saw his work as a chance to help others by standing by them in their need. All were amazed at the real compassion and gentleness of this teenager. With typical adolescent generosity, Juan responded to the attraction he felt toward those in need and repressed the revulsion that welled up in him as he washed the hideous sores and saw the human anguish in the faces of the patients.

As a person of great tenderness and sensitivity, Juan shared what others suffered. He was one of those whose heart goes out immediately to others and whose lives are dominated by their love of other people in great pain. Being close to the destitute taught Juan the real values of life; he found the key to growing up, to becoming a man. He did not see the patients as the objects of his apostolic zeal. He saw them first and foremost as people. He respected them because he discovered that the way they related to him and to each other taught him about life. They sensitized him to the beauty and ugliness of life. Juan found and related to God, the suffering God and the celebrating God, precisely in relating to them.

Yet he recoiled at some of their diseases. At times he tired of the constant drudgery involved and just wanted to be alone. The times he found to study in the loft of a barn that was part of the hospital complex were the ones he treasured and sought out as pure relief from the constant pressure of his work. When Don Alvarez, who had taken quickly to him, offered to let him pursue his education at the newly founded Jesuit school, Juan was thrilled.

Besides learning more about grammar, rhetoric, and metaphysics at school, Juan met a young Jesuit, hardly older than himself, who became his teacher. Fray Juan Bonifacio became a friend as well as a mentor to young Juan. They discussed the young boy's fears and the difficulties of his demanding life as a student-orderly. Fray Juan Bonifacio gave his eager student a serious grounding in the Latin and Spanish classics that took Juan beyond an elementary level.

Partly as a result of Bonifacio's friendship and intellectual stimulation, Juan began to reflect on his life during the four years of his studies (1559–1563). He was puzzled by the poverty of his family, the death of his father, the strength of his mother, the suffering and inner strength of the people he nursed at the hospital. But amid his confusion and even though he was an adolescent, he realized that the events of his life had meaning. He knew that God was involved in it although he was not sure how. Only at the end of his lifetime would he be able to see how everything fitted together to form a pattern.

But if Juan reflected on his life and daydreamed about his future, it was not because he had a lot of idle time on his hands. His scholastic work and nursing kept him busy, but he had other duties as well. Since the hospital was for the poor, the patients could contribute little if anything to its upkeep. Funds had to be found somewhere. Since its foundation almost a hundred years earlier, one or more of the hospital staff had gone out into the city to beg. They made a special effort to collect funds during the trade fairs.[9] When Juan began to work, this was one of his jobs. People would put money or donations in kind (bread, grain, food, cloth, candle wax and the like) into his basket. This was a new experience for him. Though his own family had been very poor, they had never had to go out and beg for help. So he found this part of his duties very hard. It was only the love that this sensitive young man had for the people who depended upon him that gave him the courage to pester people for donations. He was determined to make a success of his begging, and the experience helped him to come to know himself a little better.

Juan's own situation was not better than that of the patients he comforted. His sleeping accommodations were perfectly miserable! His "room" was simply a corner with a few twigs and branches spread across the floor. Yet he kept himself neat and clean. His concern for cleanliness, typical of Juan throughout his life, was quite unusual in an age when people bathed only a few times a year. The only quiet place where he could have some privacy to study and to think about his life was a loft infested with bugs. His mother found him there one day so absorbed in his reading that he was oblivious to the insects crawling around him. The time he spent at the hospital at Medina del Campo taught him the meaning of asceticism — to be free from all things in order to love them all the more deeply and truly, even passionately.

Juan developed in the few years he worked at the hospital. Although he was to remain small in stature — about four feet ten inches — his spirit grew and his personality developed. His love for others and his concern with the alleviation of their suffering became more and more important. God was a "natural" part of everyday life in sixteenth-century Spain, but he was more than this to young Juan de Yepes. God was becoming his intimate friend. Indeed, he had fallen in love with God. As he struggled with the troublesome aspects of growing up, he lost sight of God and then rediscovered Him and learned to communicate with God more deeply as God did with him — in all the daily events of his life.

When he was twenty-one years old, Juan began to think of making another kind of life for himself. It was about this time that he was approached by Don Alvarez, who had another offer to make to him. Alvarez wanted him to be ordained as chaplain to the hospital. His role would be to say Mass and serve the patients in a sacramental way. This opened new possibilities for Juan and for his family as well. If he accepted the offer, he would finally be able to give his mother more substantial help. He certainly would not be rich, but he would have the means to give her a chance to rest a little. It would also mean he could continue to help the sick, not only physically as he had done until now, but spiritually as well. It would be easy since he knew the hospital with its doctors and nurses. It would be fascinating, he thought, and he already liked the work. The more he thought about all this, the clearer it was that this could very well be the ideal place for him. Yet there was something within him that resisted the offer. Finally, after much thought, he decided that the chaplaincy at Las Bubas was not for him.

Around 1560 the Carmelites had founded a monastery called the Convento de Santa Ana in Medina del Campo. In

1563 when Juan finished his program of studies with the Jesuits, he made up his mind to join these Carmelites. For one reason or another, he did not tell Don Alvarez about his decision, but secretly left the hospital and went to the monastery where he was admitted immediately. On that warm day, as he walked toward the Carmelite monastery, he thought about his past life and his future. All that he had been given, the events, the people filled his mind. He was too gentle and sensitive not to remember those gifts of the past as he began a new direction in his life. But was it really new?

When he arrived at the small monastery, Juan asked to be received in their community. Then and there the superior clothed him with the habit and gave him the tonsure to mark his new clerical state. Thus he began his year of novitiate right away. While little is known of this year-long training within the tradition of the order of Carmel, we do know that the monastery at this time was only a small house. Juan's room was tiny, narrow and dark. During this year of novitiate, Juan practiced the rule of the community very strictly: abstinence, fasting, all night vigils, discipline, and prayer. His determination and devotion made him diligent in the practice of religious life, and he seemed to impress those who knew him with his simplicity and the consistent care he took even in the least important of tasks.

But whenever he could, he sought out solitude. He needed the pleasure of being with people, but he also needed to be alone and quiet. Both facets of life constituted important dimensions of growth for his own personality and spiritual life. Because of this deep love for silence and solitude, Juan's brothers in the community considered him somewhat strange. Since his severity held him apart from the others, he did not really become part of the group. So, while they admired him, they also thought that he was too devout. In later years when he had become a superior this early reputation preceded him and made many of the brothers fear his appointment because they thought he would be too severe. But they discovered that this austere beginning had produced a different kind of person than they had been expecting.

The year of novitiate ended much too quickly for Juan. Profession of vows took place sometime after May 21, 1564.[10] In the very same year, the Very Reverend Father Rubeo became superior general of the order. Fray Juan de Santo Matía (as he was now known in the Carmelites) celebrated his commitment to this community in the presence of the superior of Santa Ana (Padre Alonso Ruiz) and Don Alonso Alvarez, his friend and the administrator of the hospital. A new phase in Juan's life began.

NOTES

1. José Gomez-Menor Fuentes, *El linaje familias de santa Teresa y de san Juan de la Cruz: sus parrentes toledanos.* (Toledo: 1970), pp. 22–67. In this period, even if it was not absolutely necessary to hide one's Jewish ancestry because of the religious and social restrictions that this would place upon any of the descendants, it was wise to do so. For more detailed descriptions of the situation, see also Stephen Clissold, *St. Teresa of Avila* (London: Sheldon Press, 1979), pp. 1–13; Teofanes Egido, "The Historical Setting of St. Teresa's Life" in *Carmelite Studies* I (1981): 122–182.

2. José Gomez-Menor Fuentes, *El linaje familias de santa Teresa y de san Juan de la Cruz: sus parrentes toledanos*, p. 43.

3. Jeronimo de San José, *Historia del Venerable Padre Fray Juan de la Cruz Primer Descalzo carmelita, compañero y Coadjutor de Santa Teresa de Jesús en la Fundación de su Reforma* (Madrid: Diego Diaz de la Carrera, 1641), p. 12. The date is uncertain. He might have been born either on the feast of John the Baptist in June or on the feast of John the Evangelist in December. This specification of the feast day is deduced from the fact that his name was Juan and that he might have been given the name because of the feast day on which he was born, as was common at that time. Unfortunately, a fire in the parish church destroyed the records of his baptism.

4. *Living Flame of Love-B*, 1, Crisogono de Jesús, ocd, *Vida y Obras de San Juan de la Cruz* (Revision and notes by Matías del Niño Jesús, ocd; critical edition by Lucinio del SS. Sacramento, ocd) (Madrid: Biblioteca de Autores Cristianos [BAC], 1964), p. 829. The English translation is from *The Collected Works of St. John of the Cross*, trans. Kieran Kavanaugh, ocd, and Otilio Rodriguez, ocd (Washington, D.C.: Institute of Carmelite Studies Publications, 1979), p. 578. *The Collected Works* is hereafter referred to as (Kav.). One might also wonder if the various colors

referred to in the *Spiritual Canticle-B* are not the result of a trained weaver's sensitivity to color combinations.

5. Fray José de Velasco, *Vida y virtudes y muerte del Venerable Varon Francisco de Yepes, Vezino de Medina del Campo, que murió M. DC. VII* (Barcelona: G. Margarit, 1624), p. 7.

6. Biblioteca Nacional de Madrid (BNM), Ms. 12738, fol. 613.

7. Martín Alberto Marcos, "El sistema hospitalerio de Medina del Campo en el siglo XVI" in *Cuadernos de Investigación Historica* 2 (1978), 349-351.

8. Jeronimo de San José, *Historia*, pp. 23-24.

9. Martín Alberto Marcos, "El sistema hospitalerio," p. 348.

10. Crisogono de Jesús, ocd, *Vida y Obras*, p. 45.

II

The Young Carmelite and the Reform (1564–1572)

W hen he finished his novitiate, young Fray Juan de Santo Matía travelled to Salamanca where he prepared
himself further for what was to be his new life among the Carmelites. Late in the year 1564 when the Carmelite friar arrived in the university city, Salamanca's cold winter winds
were already blowing through the narrow cobblestone
streets. This center of intellectual learning in Spain appeared
rather unwelcoming in the drab wintry season. Yet, this did
not keep Juan from taking full advantage of the appointment
for study which was now being offered him.

Salamanca vibrated with new trends and solid learning.
All Europe knew of the university's vitality. Though Latin
was supposed to be the vehicle of conversation, the new pride
which Spaniards took in their language was pushing it aside.
Changes such as this that were typical of the ferment of a
dynamic era excited the young students of literature and
philosophy. The harmonious cadences of the Castilian language made him fall in love with it. Students often composed
their own songs in this romance language. Could it be that
Fray Juan did the same? Possibly. He had entertained the sick
in Medina del Campo with his songs. We also know that in
later life he wrote a poem based on a Castilian ballad[1] and
that he often sang songs as he travelled from one place to an-

other. Here in Salamanca his interest in music kept pace with his love of literature and the Spanish language. He was clearly a student who was deeply influenced by the atmosphere prevalent at the University at the time.

Only 750 of the university's 7000 students were studying theology. Noise and color filled the narrow, snakelike streets of the old city. The lay students made the noise as they joked, talked and teased each other on their way to class. This was the only time for any levity since the discipline in their own residences and the university itself was terribly rigid. All the students contributed to the rich riot of color. The major schools had special colors which the students wore. So, before and after classes the streets were filled with people wearing cloaks of gray, blue, and purple mingling with the white capes of the Carmelites and the colorful habits of the different religious communities which had houses of study in the city. The same striking melange of colors could be seen after class when a professor would stand by a pillar and answer students' questions. Fray Juan was certainly part of this inquisitive crowd for he constantly sought to understand more of the world that was unfolding before him daily.

He went to classes at the University, though he was also studying at the Carmelite Colegio of San Andrés which was situated on the banks of the Tormes river outside the city walls. The more gifted of the Carmelite friars went to the University. In 1564-1565 the register of the University noted the presence of "Fray Juan de Santo Matía natural de Medina del Campo del obispado de Salamanca," and he continued to be registered there as an arts student until 1567. In 1567-1568 he was listed as a priest and theologian.[2] He was so successful in his studies that his superior named him prefect of students with the responsibility of teaching and helping the other brothers who studied there. All these experiences helped shape the personality of Fray Juan.

In the Colegio de San Andrés, Fray Juan's living quarters

were spartan. His room was small, dark and narrow with a little window which opened onto the chapel and a small opening in the roof to let in some light. A few boards without a
mattress or pillow served as his bed. Juan conscientiously followed the stricter ancient Carmelite rule by his own choice.
Some of the other friars who neither followed a personal program of asceticism nor showed much zeal for the common
rule avoided Fray Juan because they thought him too serious,
just as in Medina del Campo his severe asceticism isolated
him from the others. His youth and zeal led him into a situation where the others considered him too strict and perhaps
even fanatical. Strangely enough it was through his studies at
Salamanca that he gradually broke out of the "angelism" to
which he was prone in this youthful period. The beauty of the
literature he studied and the various other trends of the time
could have been rejected by Fray Juan as simply earthly
things to be put aside. But his temperament was too strongly
drawn in this direction. He instinctively knew they could not
be evil, though he was not yet comfortable with the pleasure
he took in them. It was only later in life that he realized deep
in his own personality that the wholeness of our world had to
be integrated into the process of learning to love God. But
this realization was taking root even now in Fray Juan.

At twenty-two he saw himself as someone who could not escape from his aloofness no matter how he tried to be kind
toward others. He was determined, silent and studious. In
fact, we could say he did not seem to be a very pleasant person to have around. If some of the brothers were speaking
when they should have been silent and he came along, they
would run away immediately because they knew that if they
stayed he would give them a little sermon about the rule. In
fact, the other friars avoided him whenever possible. Thus
Fray Juan was alone a good deal of the time. Was this really
the Juan of the Hospital de Las Bubas? Yes, but a real lack of
balance in his attitudes and activities had developed. He still

perceived spiritual life as "spiritual" or otherworldly and consequently he developed a severe, harsh attitude toward earthly life. His determination to follow the rule strictly did not endear him to his fellow students. He was one of the fervent types to be found in any novitiate or scholasticate—filled with a desire to be holy but with an inhuman notion of what holiness is.

However, in Juan this was simply too contrary to his sensitive nature to last very long. The fascination and beauty of the real world around him drew him too strongly for him to deny its goodness. It gnawed at him and in an effort to end his yearning he increased his ascetical practices as if they could free him of all this earthliness. Consciously he may have felt it was necessary to get out of the world through disciplining his body, fasting, vigils, and long prayers. But unconsciously he was discovering how incarnate he was and how necessary this was to become one with the God of Jesus. His Salamancan period was not wasted. His coming to God utilized all the learning experiences of his life.

By 1567, Fray Juan de Santo Matía was sufficiently advanced in his studies to be ordained. In August of that year, he returned to Medina del Campo for the celebration of his first Mass among his relatives and the friends of his earlier days. The trip from Salamanca to Medina del Campo, though not long, provided him with time for some serious thinking. Fray Juan had long been reflecting on the possibility of adopting another life-style. The life at Carmel did not seem strict enough for him. He was not passing judgment on others. He simply wanted to make more than the little effort the rule of Carmel demanded of him.

While in Salamanca he had nurtured a secret desire. No doubt the isolation from the others which his own practices led him into played its role here too. Since he was unable to communicate freely with his fellow Carmelites in San Andrés, solitude was more or less imposed on him. It was natural that he should begin to feel alienated from a group with whom he could not share his hopes and ideals. This sense of not belonging had been growing in him ever since his novitiate days. The little friar had not really made friends in his Carmelite community. For such a sensitive man, this was a heavy cross. To be unable to share his intimate hopes or desires with a like-minded friend must have been extremely painful. But, since he had not yet become the open and loving person he was to be later, few if any were attracted to this little "saint." His strictness excluded him from the fellowship which normally develops in such a setting. His superior intellectual abilities and his appointment as prefect effectively separated him from the group. No wonder that by the time of his first Mass, he was seriously contemplating joining the Carthusians.

Juan's hopes settled on the Monasterio del Paular, which was situated near Segovia. Here he felt he could live out the saintly life as he then saw it; i.e., he could spend his life withdrawn from "worldly commerce," quiet and alone with God. Community life was not even accentuated so he felt he would be quite happy. No longer would he have to be different from the others. Most of all, he could devote himself entirely to God. But could the young man who had given himself completely to the sick in Las Bubas and to the students at San Andrés really isolate himself even for God? Perhaps even now he saw that this God is not just in the infinite beyond. Rather God came and comes in time and in people. This realization was surely in the back of Juan's mind as he thought about his future. Although going to Paular seemed right, something was amiss about it. His companion, Fray Pedro de Orozco, whom he had taken with him to Medina del Campo, knew that Fray Juan had to meet la Madre Teresa de Avila. Therefore, he arranged the meeting which would be a key event in the history of the order of Carmel and of Christian mysticism.

On August 14, 1567, *La Madre*, as she was called, went to
Medina del Campo to establish her second monastery of sisters. There were some difficulties in getting a house for them,
but these were gradually overcome. It is as she spoke about
this that we understand what transpired during her meeting
with Fray Juan de Santo Matía:

> With all this happening, I began to be easier in my mind; for
> we were completely enclosed where we were, and we began to
> say the Hours, while the good Prior (Fray Antonio de Heredia)
> took up the matter of the house with all speed, and went to
> great trouble about it. He said that, in spite of everything, it
> would not be finished for two months; but it was so well done
> that we were able to stay there with reasonable comfort for
> several years .... While I was there, I was continually preoc-
> cupied about monasteries for friars; and having no friars, as I
> have said, I did not know what to do. So I resolved to discuss
> the matter in the strictest confidence with the Prior there, and
> see what advice he would give me. I did this: he was very glad
> when he heard of it and promised me that he would be the
> first to join us. I took that for a joke and told him so; for al-
> though, besides being a learned man, he was a good friar, giv-
> en to recollection, very studious and fond of his cell, he did not
> seem to me to be at all the man for the beginning of an enter-
> prise of this kind; he had not sufficient spirituality, nor could
> he have endured the necessary privations, being delicate in
> health and not accustomed to them. But he reassured me
> most earnestly and told me that for a long time the Lord had
> been calling him to a stricter life, that he had already resolved
> to go to the Carthusians and that they had assured him that
> they would receive him. Nonetheless, though very glad to hear
> this of him, I was not quite satisfied: I asked him, therefore, to
> let us wait a while so that he might practice the things which
> he would have to promise to do .... [3]

Not long after that, sometime in September or October,
Madre Teresa de Jesús had heard of Fray Juan de Santo Matía

from his companion, Fray Pedro de Orozco. Fray Pedro arranged a meeting within that two-month period.

Madre Teresa was already fifty-two years old and had long
been involved in the establishment of the reform of the
female section of the order of Mt. Carmel. Her ideal was to
establish some monasteries where the nuns would follow the
primitive rule rather than the mitigated one which all had
followed before her movement started. She had recently
received permission from the Superior General of the Order,
Padre Juan Bautista Rubeo (Rossi) to start two convents of
the reform, in addition to the Convento de San José she had
founded several years earlier in Avila. Medina del Campo
was the first of these new convents. The excerpt quoted from
her *Foundations* shows that she was anxious to start the
reform of the male part of the order.

The primitive rule of the Carmelites was rather strict, but
it had been made easier through the centuries as zeal dimin-
ished and as the accent shifted from a more contemplative
basis to an apostolic orientation. Pope Eugenius IV mitigated
the rule in 1432 and other popes lightened it even more.
Teresa decided to return to the primitive rule which, among
other things, made contemplative prayer and silence the
most important features of the life-style. Total abstinence
from meat and lengthy fasting from September 14 (the feast
of the Exaltation of the Holy Cross) to Easter were reinstated
in the reform movement of Teresa. Part of the reform also involved a change in the religious dress. Rather than the graceful, soft and full habits of the Carmelites of the mitigated
rule, the nuns and later the friars of Teresa's reform would
wear a shorter, less ample habit made of a coarse, heavy
material. Furthermore, they would no longer wear shoes as
the mitigated rule allowed. Thus the reform monks and nuns
came to be known as Discalced friars and nuns while the
others were known popularly as the Calced. While the nuns
of the reform would remain cloistered, the friars would con-

tinue to be committed to an apostolic activity consisting of preaching, celebrating the liturgy, and spiritual direction, though it was Teresa's intention that they maintain a deeply contemplative life-style. This was her hope for the future as she met with Fray Juan de Santo Matía.

This young friar, who was only twenty-five years old at the time, was bent upon becoming part of a community that would be more austere and thus more to his liking. He was bound to be fascinated by the goals of Madre Teresa. Madre Teresa has left us a description of their quiet meeting:

> Shortly afterwards there happened to arrive a young Father who was studying in Salamanca. With him was a companion (Fray Pedro de Orozco) who told me great things about the life which that Father was leading. His name is Fray Juan de la Cruz. I praised Our Lord; and when I spoke to the friar, I liked him very much; he told me that he too was preparing to go to the Carthusians. I described to him what I had in view and begged him earnestly to wait until the Lord gave us a monastery, pointing out what a great blessing it would be, if he were destined for a higher life, that he should lead it within his own Order, and how much better service he would thus render to the Lord. He gave me his word to do this provided that there were no long delay. When I saw that I had two friars to make a beginning with, the thing seemed to me settled, although I was still not quite satisfied with the Prior. So, for this reason, and also because I had as yet no place to begin in, I waited for some little time.[4]

She was excited at the prospect of having this young, determined friar as part of the reform. Fray Juan continued to impress her over the years, though not always in a comfortable way. He was as strong and determined as she was. Though she did not realize it immediately, it was not long before she came to see that she had finally met her match in a man. All the other men she had met simply were overwhelmed by her

presence and her abilities and acceded to her wishes with respect and admiration. Fray Juan de Santo Matía on the
other hand would clearly inform her of his opinion whether
or not it agreed with hers.[5] She herself said as early as 1568
that he irritated her and that they sometimes had arguments
when their opinions differed.[6] It is not surprising therefore
that though she knew Juan would be a most faithful and
helpful servant of the reform, she chose another protegé to
be the superior: Fray Jeronimo de la Madre de Dios (Gracian). This young, energetic, handsome man who had a very
real zeal for the community was especially perfect in La
Madre's eyes, because he always agreed with her. Fray Juan
was the only one she could never really control. No doubt
Teresa appreciated him for this reason, but at the same
time, she did not want him in a position where his ideas
could cause her difficulties. Nonetheless Fray Juan was to
become an essential part of the reform as a result of this
meeting. Initially however, this new turn in his life had to be
kept quiet.

Fray Juan returned to Salamanca to study theology in November of 1567. Madre Teresa, meanwhile, busied herself establishing other houses and getting ready for the new one
which would house the men of the reform. By May of 1568, a
Señor Rafael Mejia gave her a "house" at Duruelo, not far
from Avila. Towards the end of June, Teresa went to see it
with a companion. Her description of the twenty-five-mile
journey and what she saw is remarkable:

> Although we set out early in the morning, we were unfamiliar
> with the road and so went astray; and, as little is known of the
> place (Duruelo) we could find no one to direct us. We trav-
> elled all that day in the greatest discomfort, for the sun was
> very strong. When we thought we were near the village, we
> found we had as far again still to go. I always remember the
> fatigue of that long round-about journey. We arrived only a
> little before nightfall. When we entered the house, we found it

in such a condition that we dared not spend the night there, so dirty was it and so numerous were the harvesters who were about. It had a fair sized porch, a room divided into two, with a loft above it, and a little kitchen: that is all there was of the building which was to be our monastery. I thought that the porch might be made into a church, that the loft would do quite well for the choir and the friars could sleep in the room below. But my companion, though a much better person than I am and a great lover of penance, could not bear the thought of my founding a monastery there. "Mother," she said, "I am certain that no one, however good and spiritual, could endure this. You must not consider it." The Father who was travelling with me, though he thought as she did, made no objection when I told him what was in my mind. We went and spent the night in the church, but so great was our fatigue that we would not spend it in vigil.[7]

This rather depressing hovel was to be the new home and the beginning of the reform for Fray Juan de Santo Matía. But first he needed to talk with Teresa about the new spirit of the community he was about to start.

For Fray Juan 1567-1568 was a long year of waiting. He had just had time to have a brief meeting with La Madre in late October 1567 before she was obliged to leave Medina del Campo to regulate the affairs of the reform. Teresa's departure left Juan and Fray Antonio with a few days of leisure before they were expected to return to Salamanca. They used the time to discuss their hopes for the success of the reform and to plan the life they were to share. They differed in age and personality. Fray Juan was more retiring and quiet, while Fray Antonio was outgoing and talkative. As they spoke, they found that more and more the ideal of living the primitive rule delighted them both. When they considered all the circumstances, they found that they both needed the support their newly found companionship provided them. Their own talks and the ones they had had with Madre Teresa became things that Fray Juan continued to think about during his year at Salamanca. For the time being, their plans were to remain secret.

Being the conscientious and determined person that he was, Fray Juan immersed himself in his studies of theology. The professors who taught at Salamanca had the perfect student in this small friar. He was not one to simply accept what a professor told him. He would reflect upon the ideas presented, search out the texts, and study them carefully. Over the years he had developed his studies in such a serious and exacting way that they had become a form of prayer.

Juan spent his last year in Salamanca restlessly waiting for the reform to start. The cloisters and their ornate facades had lost their appeal. Self-doubt clouded his anticipation. Would he be strong enough to live it? Was this really God's will or his own? Was he simply trying to run away from other responsibilities? The questions would come and go and come back again, but he always would take them seriously. Yet, despite the appearances, these doubts never destroyed the underlying conviction that he had that this indeed was the way in which he had to move. He sensed deep within himself that somehow this was right for him. He clung to this conviction when he returned to Medina del Campo in the summer of 1568, just after he turned twenty-six years old.

By July 1, 1568, Madre Teresa had arrived in Medina del Campo on her way from Malagon. She had already seen Duruelo and had informed both Fray Juan and Fray Antonio about its miserable condition. But this did not dampen their spirits. They wanted to get on with the new foundation so that they could finally commit themselves to this new life that they had been waiting so long to begin. Nonetheless a few more minor details had to be settled before they could embark upon this adventure. The delay, however, gave Fray Juan some time to prepare more intensely for the coming years.

He and Madre Teresa had a month to talk over the reform before they left with some others for Valladolid. During that time they discussed the basic spirit behind the reform movement that Teresa had started and Fray Juan thus received some insight into the importance and fundamental thrust behind La Madre's actions and her hopes. These discussions intensified as they travelled the twenty-eight miles from Medina del Campo to Valladolid, where the Madre hoped to establish yet another convent of her sisters.

The small group of travellers included six nuns, a young girl who was about to join them, Fray Juan himself, Madre Teresa and the former chaplain to San José (the first Discalced convent which Madre Teresa established in Avila). Each of them underwent a mini-novitiate as Madre Teresa interspersed silence and prayer with discussions about their way of life as Discalced Carmelites. This novitiate of Fray Juan continued during the following weeks as they tried to obtain the necessary authorizations to establish the monastery at Duruelo. This period became his introduction to a whole new life-style which was to be his for the next twenty-three years.

Duruelo

With the documents in hand and with a few things with which to start his new life, Fray Juan left Valladolid for Avila in early September, 1568. Not long afterward, Fray Juan and a lay-brother called Fray Joseph de Cristo left Avila on the road to Duruelo.

Though he had not officially taken the vows of the Discalced, Fray Juan already looked like one in the habit the Madre and her nuns had made him and requested that he wear. Though he was so short, he looked impressive in the coarse, dark gray-brown scapular and cassock over which he wore the modified version of the flowing white cape so familiar to those who knew the Carmelites. His dark skin, long narrow nose, and thin face topped with a receding hairline per-

fectly fit the austere clothes that he wore. The rosary hanging
from his belt clicked quietly as he and the brother walked
barefoot toward their new home.

When they arrived in Duruelo, they discovered that La
Madre's description of the place was quite accurate. It was a
rather desolate place. The surrounding fields that had already been divested of their crops were dusty and gray. They
found the building they would call a monastery to be more a
tumbled-down barn than a home. But, when Madre Teresa's
companion said, after their first visit to Duruelo, that no one
could be expected to live in a place like that, she had not
counted on the determination and strength of Fray Juan. Yet
even he would be taken aback by the condition of the place.
It was filthy and in a state of near collapse. Much needed to
be done. Fray Juan, who was always so clean and neat, sensed
a natural repulsion as he first entered these "ruins." Nonetheless, he would not be overcome by something as trivial as a
dirty, run-down house. The two new friars set to work immediately, sweeping, washing, nailing up boards, repairing
the whole structure.

But they were not about to simply rebuild. Sweeping,
washing floors, and fixing up walls would provide only the
shell. Rooms had to be set up and certain human touches like
decorations appropriate to their life-style had to be put into
place. Someone who knew Fray Juan very well and lived with
him later in his life describes what the two of them did to the
house in these words:

> It had only a porch and a double room with an attic and a
> small kitchen with its own entrance. They remodelled it in this
> way. They made the porch into the church. The lower room
> they made into a dormitory leaving space near the church
> part for two confessionals . . . . In the dormitory they put their
> beds which, for better or worse, were no more than straw and
> an old blanket placed on the floor while for pillows they used
> pieces of wood with two or three other pillows made of coarse

material filled with straw. They divided the kitchen in two parts: in one they made a refectory with a table covered with place mats for each monk . . . in the other was the kitchen and utensils. The attic they made into a choir room . . . . But when the snow came it fell into the attic itself . . . .[8]

To turn this old barn into a monastery required hard work and a good deal of time. Fray Juan decided to make sure people knew what the barn had become by putting a large wooden cross in the field in front of it and another cross on the front door. Still more crosses were put in different places in the small renovated barn, including a small paper one that Fray Juan himself put above the holy water font. In imitation of their Master, they wanted their life to be one of self-sacrifice for God and the world. It was not so much death to the world that they aimed at as the abandonment of all that hindered them from loving God in the world that He had created and loved. For Fray Juan everything in creation found its place in a freeing process in which the human person would find God more fully.

The two brothers in Carmel worked and prayed as they awaited the formal opening of their monastery. This took place on November 28, 1568. The provincial, Fray Alonso Gonzalez, had arrived the day before with Fray Antonio, who was to join the new group of Discalced men. On seeing Fray Juan already dressed in the habit of the Reform, his disappointment over the fact that Fray Juan had not waited for him bothered him. However, his sadness and anger soon passed as they gathered to celebrate the Eucharist to officially mark the beginning of the new venture.

At the end of the Mass, presided over by the provincial, Fray Juan, Fray Antonio, and Fray Joseph renounced the mitigated rule they had followed and promised to live according to the primitive rule. It was a new start and as a sign of that, they took new names. From now on Fray Juan de Santo Matía would be known as Fray Juan de la Cruz, while Fray Antonio Heredia would be called Fray Antonio de Jesús. Fray Joseph and two others also joined the community.

This group of five now began to live the new rule. Fray Antonio became prior, while Fray Juan de la Cruz was named Master of Novices. Silence formed a major part of their lives, especially between Compline (night prayer) and Prime. This provided them with an atmosphere for the contemplation they hoped to practice and foster. They spent much of their time praying privately and meditating on the law of the Lord. (This was in addition to the two hours of mental prayer which they performed in common every day.) They fasted regularly from the feast of the Exaltation of the Cross (September 14) until Easter.

Fray Juan de la Cruz was filled with a joyful peace during this time. Everything seemed perfect to him. How could anything more deeply contemplative be imagined? Fray Juan possessed the delights of a new beginning in Duruelo. Whether he was working in the fields or praying or preaching in the surrounding villages, everything seemed to fit perfectly into a harmonious pattern. While he saw God in all of this, he knew nonetheless that this could not be equated with God. In time Fray Juan would understand this even better.

The atmosphere that affected visitors when they beheld these monks in their humble monastery can be felt in La Madre's account of a rather quick visit she made there in early 1569.

> During the following lent, I passed the place on my way to our foundation at Toledo. I arrived in the morning: Fray Antonio de Jesús was sweeping out the church porch with that happy expression which never leaves him. "How is this Father?" I said to him. "Whatever has become of your dignity?" And he answered in these words, which showed me how very happy he was: "I curse the time when I had any." Then I went into the little church and was amazed to see what spirituality the Lord

had inspired there. And I was not alone in this, for two merchants, who were friends of mine, and had come as far as this with me from Medina, did nothing but weep. There were so many crosses about and so many skulls! I have never forgotten one little wooden cross, above the holy water, on which was stuck a piece of paper with a picture of Christ: it seemed to inspire greater devotion that if it had been a crucifix of the finest workmanship. The choir was in the loft, the centre of which was quite high, so that they could say the Hours, but they had to stoop very low in order to enter far enough to hear Mass. They had turned the two corners next to the church into two little hermitages; as the place was very cold these were filled with hay and they could only sit or lie in them, for the roof almost came down on their heads. The hermitages had two little windows over-looking the altar and two stones for pillows, and above these their crosses and skulls.[9]

The simplicity and poverty in which they all lived gave them a joy nothing else could give. They devoted themselves to prayer and the service of God and enjoyed it immensely. The cross, which was the sign of their liberation, could be seen everywhere reminding them of how they would grow in this new life-style.

The presence of Fray Juan's family added to his joy. Nothing could stand in the way of the intimacy the Yepes family shared. If anything, the fact that the youngest member of the family had started this new form of life drew the family even closer together. Consequently, shortly after Duruelo had become the first monastery of the reformed life, Fray Juan de la Cruz' mother, brother and sister-in-law came there to be with him. His mother cooked the meals at the little monastery while his sister-in-law washed the linens and clothes. Francisco, his brother, cleaned and arranged the rooms of the monastery.[10] Living and working there provided them with the necessities of life at a time when they were in great need. Fray Juan's love and concern for them saw to their comfort. Moreover, it meant a great deal to him to simply have them with him. His deep, constant love for his mother and brother impressed everyone.[11]

Both Fray Antonio and Fray Juan de la Cruz would go out to the surrounding towns to preach the Word to the people. When Francisco was at the monastery, he would accompany his brother on this apostolate. If their journey was a fair distance, they would take a little bread with them and eat it seated by some stream or by the roadside on their way back. Sometimes the pastor of the parish invited them both to stay and eat with him. But Fray Juan always politely refused the offer and went on his way. When asked why he did not stay, Fray Juan would reply gently but with conviction, "It is not good that I be paid for my service to God and His people."[12] His homilies reflected his own gentleness and encouraged the people to live what they believed. He wanted them to know that Jesus should be the center of their lives—neither persons nor things should take the place of Jesus in their hearts.[13]

Whatever his subject, Juan impressed the people who heard him. They often said that in some unique way they felt the very reality that he was trying to communicate to them.[14] They did not hear just words; they sensed a real participation in the thing he spoke of. To do this, a homilist has to have God alive in himself. Fray Juan de la Cruz had that gift. However, since he found the praises of the people quite embarrassing, he would attempt to leave secretly immediately after the homily so that he would avoid hearing the people's reaction. The return trip to the monastery was similar to the one going out—quiet, reflective, and prayerful. This did not mean, however, that Fray Juan de la Cruz trudged along the dirt roads of Castile with downcast eyes and a stern face. The world, even on these short forays outside the monastery, was an invitation to and an occasion for prayer. What Juan saw made him conscious that God was present not only deep within himself, but also in the world of which he felt himself a part. Juan's God was a God of creation, joyfully present in time. In Duruelo, Fray Juan de la Cruz lived the rule of Carmel. Its incarnation in every conscious moment of his life made him the holy one of the Discalced.

Mancera and Pastrana

Fray Juan de la Cruz lived and worked in Duruelo for over a year, but he was not to stay in this idyllic setting forever. In June of 1570 the whole Duruelo community moved to Mancera de Abajo. Here, about three miles from Duruelo, a wealthy man had offered the Discalced a house just when the arrival of new candidates had made the building at Duruelo much too small. Fray Juan continued to instruct the novices for a while after the transfer of the community to Mancera but it was not long before the community would need his talents in yet another monastery of Discalced friars.

Again it was the generosity of some local people that enabled the friars to open a monastery in Pastrana in 1569. The students in the university town of Alcala de Henares, not far from Madrid and only about thirty-five miles southeast of Pastrana, had heard about the life of contemplation that these monks were leading. Many of them were favorably impressed and wanted to join them. By October, 1570, the community called upon Fray Juan to go to Pastrana for a short visit to establish a novitiate there.

The trip to Pastrana provides us with some important elements for a deeper understanding of Fray Juan de la Cruz. Fray Pedro de los Angeles accompanied him. As they walked along the dusty roads chilled by the fall winds that were already starting to blow, Fray Juan gave Fray Pedro a few *platicas* or concise sayings concerning life or God or the world. They actually sounded like summaries of what Fray Juan had come to know through his own life. But even more interesting is the fact that along the way they begged people for money and food. They were not begging for themselves, however. They would take the money they collected and then disburse it along the way to the poor whom they met. Furthermore, in keeping with their idea of simplicity they would always sleep in very poor houses or barns. Even if someone offered them a decent place to spend the night or to rest, Fray Juan gently refused the offer. He possessed a very real sense of service as well as of poverty. He wanted to share the lot of the poor whom he saw about him and whom he had known all his life. Though this approach to realistic religious poverty appealed to him personally, he did not demand that others follow his example. They were free to accept offers of food and comfortable accommodations on trips outside the monastery, but Fray Juan regarded poverty as a means to break down the social barriers that religious erected between themselves and the oppressed or poor of Spain. Through his rather strict personal life-style he always remained at ease with the poor and maintained his freedom to live fully in the world. His contemplative life was not lived out of this world; on the contrary, it was based on a real love for the world. Though many in his time simply prayed for the poor, Fray Juan did something for them.

Soon after their arrival in Pastrana, Fray Juan set to work. He used his experience in Duruelo and Mancera to set up the novitiate and prepared Fray Gabriel de la Asunción to act as novice master. When he thought that everything was settled, he and his companion set out to return to Mancera. Their stay in Pastrana had lasted only about one month, but it was long enough to establish the structures needed to promote the ideal of the Discalced Carmelite Friars. He remained in Mancera until April of 1571.

Then the Discalced sent him to become Rector of the Colegio de San Cyrilo in Alcala de Henares. Here he organized the residence so that monks could live according to the primi-

tive rule of the Discalced. However, in the early spring of
1572 something came to his attention that forced him to
return to Pastrana.

The novice master there was now Fray Angel de San Gabriel. His strictness and the silly demands which he imposed on
the novices not only disturbed the monastery itself, but made
the people of the town ridicule and dislike the monks. Fray
Angel expected the novices to obey him without question. To
test their obedience he would command them to go about the
town dressed in rags and act as if they were madmen. This
conduct brought the scorn of the townspeople upon them
and the community. Fray Angel also ordered them to press
the townsfolk to come to the monastery. It was not long
before word spread; fewer and fewer candidates came to be
admitted while some novices actually left the community.
The situation, if left unchecked, could do great harm to the
new communities of Discalced friars. So, the superiors asked
Fray Juan de la Cruz to look into the matter and correct whatever had gone wrong.

On his arrival, Fray Juan began to correct the extreme asceticism that Fray Angel had ordered the novices to practice. But he did it with a great deal of diplomatic tact. He
spoke gently to the community on the real value of their lives
as monks of the primitive rule that accentuated prayer and
the cloister. Then he set about to change things. He put a
stop to all the penitential extravagances outside the monastery and moderated the penances and mortifications within
it. Fray Juan was only interested in those practices that succeeded in freeing individuals for real love and service to
God. In Fray Juan's opinion what had been going on before
had nothing to do with God; the practices had become ends
in themselves. With his concern for all, his gentleness and
his sound logic, Fray Juan de la Cruz reestablished a healthy
situation for a solid introduction to the primitive Carmelite
life. Now he was ready for a new assignment that would end

abruptly and introduce him to an experience that would color his whole life.

NOTES

1. *The Shepherd Boy*, BAC, p. 943 (Kav., pp. 722-23).
2. Crisogono de Jesús, *Vida y Obras*, p. 49.
3. Teresa de Jesús, *Book of the Foundations*, trans. E. A. Peers in *The Complete Works of St. Teresa of Jesus* (London: Sheed and Ward, 1972), vol. III, p. 14.
4. Teresa de Jesús, *Book of the Foundations*, pp. 14-15.
5. Fray Juan was to be her defender constantly throughout his lifetime. Even after Teresa's death, Fray Juan de la Cruz sided with Madre Ana de Jesús for the more humanitarian and Teresian inspiration of the rule's interpretation against Padre Doria (cf. Ildefonso Moriones, *Ana de Jesús y la herencia teresiana. ¿Humanismo cristiano o rigor primitivo?* Rome, Edizioni del Teresianum, 1968). He would seek her help and advice many times about the establishment of the reform. Moreover he was to be totally faithful to the reform as she wanted and conceived it. Nonetheless, he knew how to moderate some of Teresa's ideas and approaches.
6. See also Efren de la Madre de Dios and Otger Steggink, eds., *Obras Completas de Santa Teresa de Jesús* (Madrid: Biblioteca de Autores Cristianos, 1967). Epistolario, Carta a D. Francisco de Salcedo, Avila. Carta 13,2, p. 677. For a very fine discussion of the relationship of Madre Teresa de Jesús and Fray Juan de la Cruz, see also G. Morel, *Le sens de l'existence selon s. Jean de la Croix* (Paris: Aubier, 1961), pp. 78-97.
7. Teresa de Jesús, *Book of the Foundations*, pp. 62-63.
8. Fray Alonso de la Madre de Dios, *Vida, virtudes y milagros del santo padre Fray Juan de la Cruz, maestro y padre de la Reforma de la Orden de los Descalzos de Nuestra Señora del Monte Carmelo* (Biblioteca Nacional de Madrid (BNM), Ms. 13460), folios 23-24.
9. Teresa de Jesús, *Book of the Foundations*, pp. 66-67.
10. See also BNM Ms. 8568, fol. 371 quoted by José Gomez-Menor Fuentes, *El linaje familias*, p. 13.
11. This love that Fray Juan had for his mother and brother must be kept in mind as we read his works, particularly the following passage: "You should have an equal love for and an equal forgetfulness of all persons, whether relatives or not, and withdraw your heart from relatives as much as from others, and in some ways even more for fear that flesh and blood might be quickened by the natural love which is ever alive among kin and which must always be mortified for the sake of spiritual perfection." *The Precautions*, BAC, p. 948 (Kav., p. 656).
12. José de Velasco, *Vida virtudes y muerte del Venerable Varon Francisco*, p. 88.
13. Very likely on some such occasion he would have spoken to them words

similar to what he wrote in *The Ascent of Mount Carmel:* "Any person questioning God or desiring some vision or revelation would not only be guilty of foolish behavior but also of offending Him, by not fixing his eyes entirely upon Christ and by living with the desire for some other novelty. God could respond as follows: 'If I have already told you all things in My Word, My Son, and if I have no other word, what answer or revelation can I now make that would surpass this? Fasten your eyes on Him alone, because in Him I have spoken and revealed all, and in Him you shall discover even more than you ask for and desire . . . .'" (*The Ascent* II, 22,5, BAC pp. 450-451, Kav., p. 180). It is indeed unfortunate that we do not have copies of the sermons he gave during this time, but perhaps some things which have come to us as his maxims might have been the original foundation for some of these homilies which touched the people of the villages so deeply. For example: "Let your speech be such that no one may be offended, and let it concern things which would not cause you regret were all to know of them" (*Maxims*, no. 150, BAC, p. 969; Kav., no. 72, p. 679). "Whoever knows how to die in all will have life in all." (*Other Counsels*, BAC, no. 169, p. 970; Kav., no. 2, p. 681); "Anyone who complains or grumbles is not perfect, nor is he even a good Christian." (*Other Counsels* BAC, no. 171, p. 970; Kav., no. 4, p. 681).

   14. Alonso de la Madre de Dios, *Vida, virtudes,* I, 18 & 20, fol. 62 & 70.

III

Avila and the Monastery of the Encarnación (1572–1577)

Avila, the home of Fray Juan from 1572 to 1577, is still very much like it was in the sixteenth century. The fortified city perches on a hilltop overlooking miles of plains which separate it from the Sierra de Grados mountains in the distance. Its ancient walls and towers stand majestically against the searing summer sun. The red-tiled roofs of the churches and houses within the city add to the burnt autumn look of this marvelous medieval city. These structures speak of strength and power and determination. It is no surprise that it was the home of the Madre, the foundress of the Discalced Carmelites.

By 1571, thirty-five years had passed since she had joined the Carmel of the Encarnación. True, she had started the reform in 1561 and had, therefore, lived outside that convent most of that decade. Yet the Encarnación, which was situated outside the city walls, had been her home for a good part of her life. The monastery was so poor that the sisters often had very little to eat. Sometimes conditions got so bad that the sisters had to temporarily stay with relatives or friends in the city. Years of this regime had eroded the religious discipline of the convent. Some sisters who had been put there by their families and who, consequently, did not think much of their vocation, were quite happy to have periods of freedom outside the monastic framework. Many expressed their displeasure at Teresa de Jesús' reform. After all she had lived with them and she too had spent a good deal of time outside. Who was she to start a reform? By 1571 the convent of some 130 nuns was in desperate need of someone who could take things in hand. It was because of this whole situation that the Apostolic Commissioner, Fray Pedro Fernandez, appointed Madre Teresa de Jesús as Prioress of the Encarnación.

Everyone expected trouble. Not only had Teresa been establishing convents of the Reform for several years, but in July, 1571, she formally renounced the mitigated rule and embraced the stricter rule of the Discalced. Furthermore, she had been appointed prioress by an outsider instead of being elected by the nuns themselves as was usually done. The sisters, who were not interested in a stricter life-style and were afraid that Teresa would try to make them all follow the Discalced rule, opposed her nomination. Such things did not make for a smooth transition of authority.

Despite this, on October 6, 1571, the superior remained firm and named Teresa prioress and, as expected, she encountered a good deal of resistance. On that day a small procession of people walked from the convent of San José in the eastern section of the city, along the walls and down the hill to the Encarnación, north of the city walls. Madre Teresa de Jesús; the Provincial of the Calced Fathers, Fray Angel de Salazar; the Mayor of Avila; and some guards made up the group. When they reached the convent doors and knocked, the nuns inside shouted and screamed at them. They refused to let Teresa in and they were not about to admit any of the others either. These nuns stridently hurled their insults at Teresa and adamantly rejected her as their new prioress. The more Fray Angel attempted to calm them down, the more determined they became. The Madre sat on the stone bench outside and waited. Finally, at one point when Fray Angel pretended to leave, the shouts subsided long enough for a nun to cry out from within: "We want her." And then some entoned the "Te Deum" which threw further confusion among the nuns while the door was opened. The officials who had accompanied her could still hear arguing going on within the cloister as they returned to the city. Those against having Teresa de Jesús still screamed at her and at their opponents. Those who favored Teresa shouted back. But gradually Teresa de Jesús transformed these violent beginnings into peace and calm.

The new prioress set about trying to put order into the Convent. She obtained the appointment of Fray Juan de la Cruz as confessor to the sisters as soon as she reasonably could do so. She knew his gentleness and deep knowledge of life with God would be most helpful to this convent. The five years he spent there did in fact accomplish a great deal, though it is only human that everyone within the convent was not convinced of his wisdom even after that period of time.

It is no wonder that there was a good deal of resistance on the part of some nuns, at least, to Fray Juan's appointment. Just the previous year Teresa had been appointed, not elected, as prioress over them. While their greatest fears of being forced to follow the primitive rule had not materialized, la Madre had made things more ordered and hence more strict. Now they saw the naming of Fray Juan as just another subtle step in the direction of making them all into a strict, contemplative group. They had been Calced and had always had the guidance of their own monks, but now Teresa imposed a monk of the Discalced upon them. To heighten their fears, this Fray Juan de la Cruz had a reputation for being very severe. Things were bound to be strained not only for the few days after his arrival but for several years.

The choice of Fray Juan de la Cruz as one of the several confessors and guides in the spiritual life for the nuns of the Encarnación was a wise one indeed.[1] The nuns who suspected this appointment as a subtle edging toward the reform were not totally wrong. Teresa wanted Fray Juan nearby so that they could easily discuss the reform and more conveniently work out the difficulties involved. She also knew that with him as guide, all the sisters would gradually become more interested in a deepening spiritual life. Moreover, it was a fact that Teresa's activity in establishing reformed convents interested some of the nuns here. All of these elements combined would make the convent much more faithful at least to the mitigated rule of the Calced. However, none of this could be done without instructing them theoretically and experientially about religious life in Carmel. What better person to do this than the little friar from Castile? Fray Juan de la Cruz accepted this appointment with full awareness of its ramifications. Madre Teresa had contacted the Apostolic Visitor, the Dominican Fray Pedro Fernandez, and had obtained the necessary permission and authorizations for the appointment of two friars chosen from among the Discalced: Fray Juan de la Cruz and Fray Germán de Santo Matía. This certainly did not help smooth matters over with the Calced Fathers of the order. For years, the Calced had been the chaplains and confessors of the nuns at the Encarnación and had been paid for their services. Now, these two friars of the reform came in and, because they had the authorization of the Visitor, there was nothing that the Calced Friars could do but resign themselves to the facts. Some of them who lived in the Calced monastery on the hill were bitter. Jealousies, suspicions, and a dislike of the two friars abounded even before their arrival.

When Fray Juan and Fray Germán arrived, during the summer of 1572, they lived first with the Calced Carmelites. The Monastery of Neustra Señora del Carmen was located on the northern wall of the city. Its bell tower was clearly visible from the monastery of the Encarnación which lay just down the hill from the city walls. This meant that the guides and confessors could easily reach the monastery by taking a short walk of perhaps five or ten minutes. While this was a physically convenient arrangement, the suspicions and hatred of some of the friars at the monastery caused Fray Juan and his companion to move in 1573.

There were several small houses near the garden of the monastery that formed part of the property of the Encarnación but were not within its cloister. They were tiny buildings where workmen employed by the monastery lived with their families. These houses were right on the street and very close one to another. The two monks took up residence in one of these huts. It was a poor place with hardly any furniture, but it was in keeping with the likes of the little friar in the coarse habit of the Discalced.

For the next four years Fray Juan de la Cruz' life centered on Avila, this hut, and the monastery. Day after day he performed his usual routine tasks, but with a consciousness that made even little things seem different and important. Gradually during this period, he came to see that what had seemed in Duruelo to be the height and final stage of his personal drama was only a first step in his new life.

Day after day he performed his tasks as guide of the sisters at the Encarnación. Having already begun his day with prayer in his little house with his companion, Fray Juan would walk across the road to the monastery chapel to celebrate Mass for the community of sisters who lived there. Normally the sisters would go to confession every week or every two weeks. Thus Fray Juan kept fairly busy with this ministry alone. While this sacrament was not really spiritual direction, Fray Juan's approach to it involved giving much encouragement and advice. He was too sensitive a man to use the sacrament of penance in a merely rote way. It was for him one of the meeting places between God and the human person. As such, it needed to be celebrated with patience, compassion, and understanding. When Fray Juan was involved, it was filled with these qualities because they were personal qualities which he had received and had nurtured within himself.

It was not long before many (though not all) of the nuns discovered what a marvelous guide they had in this man. Each related to him from the particular state she herself was in at any given moment. The more serious the nuns were about their lives, the more they saw in Fray Juan a man who could help them on their way to God. Often he would give the sisters who consulted him sayings written on small pieces of paper to serve as their guideposts. These points were similar to the actual *platicas* we find in his works such as: "Seek in reading and you will find in meditation; knock in prayer and it will be opened to you in contemplation."[2] "Take neither great nor little notice of who is with you or against you and try always to please God. Ask Him that His will be done in you. Love Him intensely, as He deserves to be loved."[3] "Be silent concerning what God may have given you and recall that saying of the bride: 'My secret for myself.' Is. 24:14."[4]

Through these maxims and other means he tried to help them come to see that God was as real as the flowers in the garden. He wanted them to realize that this God touched their lives intimately, that He could be found within each person, in each life. The monastery had lost some of its sense of purpose, but Fray Juan, who had learned how to come closer to God, could offer the nuns light along the way.

Fray Juan de la Cruz' actions showed the path to God and revealed God's presence in that very path. The friars' meals were brought from the turnstile of the monastery to their hut. Fray Juan ate whatever was sent without complaint, but when he noticed that the cook had put something special on the tray, he would ask that it be taken back to the monastery and given to one of the sisters in the infirmary. This gesture was not motivated by an ascetical desire to punish his body but his love for others. As always those who were sick were the special objects of his love. Any gifts he received were treated the same way as any special food that he was offered. He would give them to those who needed them most to bolster their spirits by demonstrating that someone really cared about them. His love for others is striking. At thirty or thirty-five years of age, Fray Juan was an incredibly gentle, sensitive, and compassionate human being.

One day as he was walking in the monastery, he saw a nun who was barefoot even though she was not a member of the Discalced reform. She was not wearing shoes because the monastery did not have the money to buy her a pair. So Fray Juan went into the city of Avila to beg for money. When he had collected enough, he came back to the monastery and gave the money to the nun so she could buy a pair of shoes.

We cannot doubt that Fray Juan's attitude and activities were a result of his own life experiences in which God came to him as He comes to all human persons. Through the living out of his life, his consequent interaction with others, and his growing consciousness of God's presence, Fray Juan grew continuously into the man of God that he was meant to be.

However, during this Avilan period we should not think that Fray Juan was limited to the work of the monastery. The hut he shared with Fray Germán was very close to the other huts in which the families of the workers lived. His hermitage was in the midst of human life. Children played in the yards. Mothers shouted at them. Neighbors casually bantered across the fences and in doorways. The families here were as poor as his own had been in Fontiveros and Medina del Campo. Fray Juan had a deep interest and love for them all, for these were his kind of people. He played with the children and taught them the rudiments of reading and writing, as well as the catechism.[5] Children engaged him in conversation. These neighborly contacts made his life more normal than some might have thought. Years after his death, old people remembered the kind and tiny friar who had lived near them at the Encarnación.

Through these neighbors and others who visited or saw him occasionally in the narrow busy streets of Avila, the people of the town came to know him. Not everyone, though, understood this friar in the rough habit, whose gaunt features gave a false impression of harshness and severity. Among these who had misconceptions about him was a rich young woman from the city. It seemed that her friends were concerned that if she continued in her vain and selfish conduct she would ruin her whole life. Yet, nothing they said seemed to have much influence on her. When they persisted in urging her to see Fray Juan at the monastery, she hesitated because he seemed so severe. She brought up all kinds of reasons why she should not go. Finally, because of the insistence of her friends, she gave in to their wishes and said that she would see him to discuss her life. As she went down the hill to the monastery, she still was not convinced that this was the right thing to do. She felt deeply that he would not understand. Moreover, she believed that he would make too many demands upon her; demands that she knew she could never fulfill. All these thoughts caused her to waver. But she struggled on. Once in his presence, however, things were different from what she had expected. As she explained to Fray Juan how she felt, she began to feel more at ease. Then, to her surprise, when she had finished telling him her story, Fray Juan said that she would have no other penance other than what she had already suffered in coming to see him. Fray Juan realized how hard it had been for her to open her heart to him; he was becoming increasingly compassionate and insightful.

Fray Juan used his qualities wisely to give hope to people who thought that there was nothing left in their lives. He would show them the positive dimensions of their lives and encourage them to live in the spirit of God's love. For example, a nun from the monastery told him how awfully discouraged she was. Day after day, she reflected upon herself and how she had not been totally faithful to her life-style. She had become so entangled in negative thinking that she had convinced herself that her sins were so evil there was no hope for her. She was on the brink of despair. After explaining all her innermost fears and thoughts, she looked at Fray Juan anxiously in the silence. Fray Juan then spoke to her warmly of God's great love, which constantly forgives without question. This may have been the occasion for one of his more famous *platicas*: "At the evening of life, you will be examined in love. Learn to love as God desires to be loved and abandon your own ways of acting."[6] These words of Fray Juan produced an opening in her heart through which God's peace flooded her being. It was this personal conviction of God's love for everyone and everything that enabled Fray Juan de la Cruz to grow in his humanity and his deep concern for others, no matter who they were or what their problem was.

A second incident during Fray Juan's stay in Avila reveals another dimension of this unique individual. The event clearly impressed him a great deal since he could still vividly recount it some twenty years later. It seems that his companion had gone away for a few days, so Fray Juan was alone in his little house much of the time. One evening as he ate his meager supper, he heard someone coming through the small garden bordering his hut. As he turned from the table toward the door, he saw a beautiful young woman standing in the doorway. She lived in the city and he had seen her there as well as at the monastery church. She was such a strikingly beautiful woman that she would certainly not go unnoticed by anyone who laid eyes upon her. When she began to speak, the little friar found that her message surprised him much more than her presence. She passionately blurted out her desire to have him as her lover. It seems that she had fallen madly in love with him and wanted him to know it. Perhaps, she thought, he felt the same way about her. Hers was an act of considerable daring for a woman in sixteenth-century Spain. Would he chase her out of the place as St. Thomas Aquinas is said to have done in similar circumstances? Would he shout and scream condemnation at her for such sinful brazenness? Would he perhaps accede to her passion? In fact, he responded in none of these ways. They spoke together. What he said to her we do not know. After they had spoken she went back to her home on the hill in Avila knowing that the kind of relationship she had desired with him was impossible. Fray Juan had spoken to her calmly and gently because this was his manner of doing things. Years before he had vowed to be faithful to God and to his fellow Carmelites. And once Fray Juan had made a commitment he remained loyal to the life or person he had chosen as long as he lived. He persevered even when fidelity caused him personal difficulty and pain. This young woman saw that the friar she loved had chosen God fully. What she did not know, however, was how Fray Juan felt as he spoke those calming words to her. When he narrated this story to his friend Fray Juan Evangelista in the last years of his life, Fray Juan de la Cruz told him how utterly appealing he had found this young woman to be. He had been very attracted to her in every way.[7] This story reveals to us a man, a human being who was able to live within his own flesh, committed to the One whom he had chosen years earlier, no matter what the circumstances. However, it was never a simple thing for him, as it is not for any human person. Passions, desires, mortality, human circumstances are the stuff in which commitment takes root and is made. Fray Juan grew into the deeply human person he was not by denying this life and all that comprises it. He grew by acknowledging and living this life more and more consciously. It was not easy, but he tried continuously. And, no doubt, he, like all human persons, failed as he struggled along the way to God.

It was because he too had feelings and passions that he was able to help others through painful periods in their lives. While he was in Avila, a nun was deeply, passionately involved with a man in the city. After a while her behavior and her inability to change bothered her immensely. After speaking with Fray Juan, she finally renewed her original commitment to God, but this infuriated her friend in the city. Moreover, he knew that the one to blame for her change of attitude was the young confessor of the Encarnación. The man was not about to let that little friar get away with such a thing. One evening after Fray Juan had heard the sisters' confessions, he began to walk back to his nearby hut. Suddenly someone burst out of the shadows and severely beat him. Though he was still swollen and bruised a few days later, he refused to say who it was who had done this thing to him. He would only say that it was right that he should suffer in his service of God. He also wanted to save difficulties for that man and the nun. He was indeed an amazingly sensitive and faithful man.

Fray Juan de la Cruz did not spend the entire time he lived at the monastery of the Encarnación in prayer. He would occasionally be called upon to travel to other convents where he was needed for one reason or another. One of these visits was in response to an appeal to exorcise a nun in Medina del Campo. After meeting her, he told the superiors that she was not possessed, but simply was suffering from a mental illness. In an age when fear of possession and of evil spirits abounded, it took a very balanced and insightful person to see clearly and steer people away from supernatural explanations of purely natural things.

During this visit to Medina del Campo he spent some time with someone he loved very much. His mother and brother were still living in Medina del Campo at the time. Knowing how much he loved her, it is certain that he would not have gone to this city without stopping to spend at least a little time with her.[8] No doubt he spoke with her about his life with the Discalced and the happiness he was enjoying despite the difficulties the community was encountering.

The events of another trip show the frustration the Discalced had to put up with as they tried to establish new houses. In mid-March 1574, Fray Juan went with Madre Teresa de Jesús, Fray Julian de Avila and a few others to establish a convent in Segovia. Though they did not have the written permission of the bishop, he had nonetheless told them they could open a convent of Discalced Carmelite nuns. This they planned to do on March 19, 1574, the feast of St. Joseph. However, when they arrived, they found that the bishop was away. The Madre instinctively feared that the Vicar-General would object to the establishment of the convent if they could not produce written authorization. Consequently, Teresa arranged to have Fray Julian of Avila celebrate a very early morning Eucharist and to have Fray Juan celebrate a second mass later. This would constitute the actual establishment of the monastery and nothing more could be done to change it. (Teresa tended to use a variety of ruses when she did not have all the necessary papers and authorizations.) However, it was not to go as smoothly as she had hoped.

When the Vicar-General heard about the early morning events, he was understandably furious at what had taken place a two minute walk away from the imposing cathedral with its gates guarded by stone lions. He charged down the slight incline to the monastery door. He made such a din that Fray Julian ran and hid, while Madre Teresa and Fray Juan were left alone to greet the angry diocesan official. He shouted out his orders: "The Blessed Sacrament is to be consumed. The decorations of this so-called chapel are to be removed and a guard placed at the door to prevent any further Eucharistic celebrations." He even threatened to put Fray Juan de la Cruz in jail for helping to establish such a monastery within the Segovian jurisdiction. But despite all this, Fray Juan remained calm. The Madre tried to explain all of it to the Vicar-General. He really was no match for her as she was never one to give in quickly or easily. After a few days the affair was settled and soon the small convent was well on its way to taking root in this beautiful ancient Roman city of Spain.

During the week or so that he was here Fray Juan took the opportunity to walk through the woods just outside the city. There he could be alone to reflect and pray. As he progressed down the steepening slope of Segovia toward the Alcazar palace where Isabella had been crowned queen almost 100 years earlier, he sensed that this place would call him back again. Past the palace towers which pierced the bright blue Segovian sky, far below the steep cliff, he saw the glittering waters of the Eresma river wending its way around the rocky precipice upon which the palace itself was built like a huge Spanish galleon sailing into infinite blue space. He could still hear the waters from the river gurgling and rushing through the valley as he climbed the opposite hillside where flocks of sheep grazed during the summer months. Mid-March was still cold and patches of snow remained here and there. However, it was easy to image the pastoral scene of summer. The natural beauty of the Segovian countryside impressed itself upon the mind and the imagination of Fray Juan de la Cruz. Fray Juan's sensitivity to nature's beauty stored these sights in his memory to rest there until he would someday call them forth to make his poetry.

He matured during his time in Avila. While others busily established monasteries for men and some for women, he kept to his more restricted work of administering the sacraments for the sisters at the Encarnación, teaching the children and giving spiritual guidance to various people. Though he fasted as the rule directed and lived out his vow of poverty in real poverty, the extreme ascetical practices he indulged in earlier were gone. He attempted to develop his sense of prayer, his consciousness of God's continual presence in himself and the world around him. When he was not actively ministering to the nuns or the people of the city, he would write snippets of poetry or carve figures of Christ crucified or some other object which would remind him of God's coming to mankind to live with His people. It was during this period that after many months of prayer and reflection, Fray Juan had a unique insight into the crushing agony of Jesus on the cross. As a result of this penetration into the mystery of Jesus' own suffering and every human person's own relationship to it, Fray Juan drew a unique sketch of it. The same three-inch-long sketch can be seen today in a reliquary at the monastery of the Encarnación. We see Christ crucified, but the view is from above. The body is weighed down, drooping earthward. Drops of blood drip clearly from his hands and head. What one sees here is a broken body, lifeless yet life-giving. This is what Fray Juan saw in his own heart. This is what he felt. This insight into Christ's own life-producing suffering and death was certainly a grace which would serve him well in the coming months.

The reform which Teresa de Jesús had started was now beginning to cause serious problems. The Carmelite family, as was to be expected, was slowly being divided by the various factions which arose in the order as a result of the reform group. Some disliked what was happening, while others felt that those wanting to live according to the more strict rule were getting too strong. Still others were jealous. However, the difficulties which grew day by day cannot be attributed entirely to those who did not wish to follow the primitive rule. The Discalced group did contain some very strong and even some obnoxious personalities. Some of Teresa's own means of establishing the reform were sometimes suspicious if not downright devious. A serious conflict was to be expected. And interestingly enough, the actual eruption was brought to a head by the actions of someone who was not even a part of the order.

Two Dominicans had been appointed Apostolic Commissioners: one for the north of Spain (New and Old Castile) and one for the south (Andalusia). Their appointment conferred upon them great powers over the order of Mount Carmel. Fray Francisco de Vargas, the Commissioner for Andalusia, was not as sensitive as Fray Pedro Fernandez for Castile. Fernandez worked closely with the different people involved while Vargas forced the issues. For example, Vargas took one house in Huelva from the Calced friars and gave it to the Discalced. Then he authorized the foundation of houses in Sevilla, Granada and La Peñuela for the Discalced. This he did despite the fact that the Carmelite Superior General, Padre Rubeo, had expressly forbidden the setting up of houses of the Reform in Andalusia.

Naturally enough, these actions caused great fears among many of the Calced Carmelites. Therefore, in early 1574 they decided to send representatives to Rome to seek the cancellation of the powers of the Apostolic Commissioners. By August 3, 1574 they were in possession of a papal document which took away the rather wide-sweeping powers of the Commissioners. However, Ormaneto, who was the Papal Legate in Spain, heard of the document. Then by his own authority as pope's representative, he appointed the same two Dominicans "Reformers" with even greater powers on December 27, 1574.

The Calced Carmelites were understandably very angry. To them the reform seemed like total rebellion. So they decided to discuss the whole matter at the General Chapter of the order to be held in May, 1575 at Piacenza, Italy. Meanwhile, Padre Rubeo wrote to Madre Teresa to ask her to explain what was happening. Since she did not receive the letter until June, 1575, she was not able to respond before the Chapter had already deliberated on the problem. Not knowing she had not yet received the Superior General's letter, the members of the Chapter thought that she was simply being headstrong and rebellious.

As part of the corrective measures which the Chapter wanted to establish, they appointed a special Visitor for

Spain and Portugal. It was decided that Padre Jeronimo Tostado would be the perfect man for the position. By mid-1576 he had arrived in Spain, but because of the conflict between his papers and the orders of the Papal Legate, the Royal Council did not grant him the necessary permission to fulfill his mandate. So Tostado left for Portugal to do his work there while awaiting the settlement of the Spanish permissions.

In the meantime, the Discalced called a meeting to begin on September 9, 1576 at Almodovar del Campo. Within the community of the Discalced there were two tendencies to be discussed: one toward a contemplative living and the other more toward apostolic living. After a long debate during which Fray Juan de la Cruz defended the more contemplative life-style, the group chose to accent the apostolic life. With this question over, they then turned their attention to their relationship with the Calced Fathers. They made a real attempt to pacify the Calced friars and among the things they decided to do was to remove Fray Juan from his position as confessor at the Encarnación. They felt that this would alleviate some of the friction between the Calced and themselves. (However, either because the nuns intervened or because the Nuncio himself reappointed Fray Juan, he continued in his work at the Encarnación.) Despite their good intentions, the problems between the two groups could not be solved immediately. Only complete separation would ultimately take care of most of these problems.

Even before the 1576 meeting, things had deteriorated to such an extent that early in 1576, the first public arrest of Fray Juan took place. The Prior of the Calced friars of Avila publically took Fray Juan de la Cruz and his companion from their hermitage. The Calced brought them as prisoners to the monastery at Medina del Campo where Fray Juan had been a novice. The Calced not only felt they were in a strong enough position to do this but they believed that they were perfectly justified. What they had not realized was the popular support which Fray Juan had behind him as a result of his ministry to the people of the area. Upon hearing what had happened, the people of Avila became very angry and sought the intervention of the Papal Legate, Ormaneto. He ordered the immediate release of Fray Juan de la Cruz. Furthermore, he forbade any Calced friar from doing anything at the monastery of the Encarnación. (Up to this time, some Calced friars still acted as confessors for the nuns there.) The Calced could not do anything but obey. Yet the resentment they harbored in their hearts gave warning that the battle was not yet finished. The actions of the Legate had made sure that the differences between the two groups would not be settled immediately.

Fray Juan was not directly involved in all the disputes, but he had a certain reputation which made him the particular object of the Calced efforts to stop the reform. All the disputes and the direction of the Discalced group was taking its toll on him. He appeared thinner than usual. He was very tired. His face was drawn. He continued to try to do his ministry as if nothing was happening. Outwardly, except for these physical appearances, he was very much the same. Those who saw him did not realize the heavy burdens he carried. He was so sensitive that the animosity and bitterness he saw and felt around him made him suffer greatly. His insight into the cross of Jesus came as a result of his own crushing pain at seeing the ongoing fights among brothers. Things had changed from the early, peaceful days at Duruelo just some eight years earlier. And it was not over yet. Far from it. Ormaneto, the Papal Legate who had been so favorable to the Discalced friars, died on June 18, 1577. He would no longer be able to protect the leaders of the reform with his papal authority. The gates were now open to the opponents and the Calced friars lost no time in bringing the reform to its knees. They viewed the whole movement now as revolutionary and rebellious. There might have been some of the Calced who saw the reform as good and sincere, but more saw its dangers and obstinacy. For the good of the Church, for peace and order, they thought it best to control or perhaps to stop this new movement entirely. They too were sincere and honest. This point of view was confirmed with the appointment of the new Papal Legate, Filippo Sega. By the time he arrived in Spain from Rome he had already spoken with the Calced superiors in the Eternal City and was not therefore favorably disposed toward the Discalced.

So it was in this atmosphere that the Calced performed their most daring act, which was to inaugurate the most influential period in the life of Fray Juan de la Cruz.

NOTES

1. Nicolás González Y González, *El Monasterio de la Encarnación de Avila*, Vol. I. (Avila: Caja Central de Ahorros y Prestamos de Avila, 1976), pp. 295-302.

2. *Maxims*. BAC no. 157, p. 969 (Kav. no. 79, p. 680).

3. *Maxims*. BAC no. 154, p. 969 (Kav. no. 76, p. 679).

4. *Maxims*. BAC no. 152, p. 969 (Kav. no 74, p. 679).

5. Nicolás González y González, *El Monasterio de*, p. 312.

6. *Sayings of Light and Love*, BAC no. 59, p. 963 (Kav. no. 57, p. 672).

7. Silverio de Santa Teresa, ocd, ed., *Obras de San Juan de la Cruz. Doctor de la Iglesia*. (Biblioteca Mistica Carmelitana, Burgos: Tipografia de "El Monte Carmelo," 1931). (Hereafter referred to as BMC) Relacion de Fray Juan Evangelista, Vol. 13, p. 389. (BNM Ms. 12738, ca. fol. 559) Since the editor does not give the Ms. pages in the printed text, I attempt to give the approximate folio number in ( ).

8. Crisogono de Jesús, *Vida y Obras*, pp. 84-85.

IV

The Dark Night of Imprisonment in Toledo (1577–1578)

The year was drawing to a close, and it was a welcomed event for Fray Juan. The pressure of the Calced Fathers was increasing day by day as they sought to control, if not end, the reform movement. The Legate who favored the Discalced had died and was replaced by one who was more antagonistic to these "rebellious monks." Though its decrees were still partially held in abeyance, the Council of Piacenza, which had been held two years earlier, hung over both Calced and Discalced like a cloud of foreboding. Even at the Encarnación things were terribly disturbed. In December, 1577, some nuns there were still under excommunication because they insisted on having Madre Teresa de Jesús as their prioress instead of another who had been named by the authorities. Tension was everywhere and Fray Juan de la Cruz felt it too. His frailty was even more evident than usual. He was exhausted, but he was not about to have a rest.

The Calced monks were also distressed. For years now they had allowed and sometimes even encouraged the reform started by Madre Teresa to continue. It had already been nine years since the first monastery for men in the reform had been opened at Duruelo. But in the meantime the Discalced had gone too far. They had established houses in Andalusia even though that had been expressly forbidden by the General. The Visitors and Commissioners appointed by the Papal Legate had gone against the wishes of the Generalate and the Chapter of the community. Though by this time Fray Juan was not directly involved in the governing of the Discalced, the Calced considered him to be one of the key figures of the reform. Padre Jeronimo de la Madre de Dios (Gracian) was certainly more deeply involved in the establishment of the Discalced, especially since Ormaneto appointed him as Visitor to the Calced in Andalusia and "Provincial Superior" of the Discalced in August, 1575. Despite the activity of men like Gracian, the Calced focused their attention on Fray Juan. Though comparatively inactive now, he was still closely associated with Madre Teresa, and being one of the founding fathers at Duruelo, he had symbolic primacy in their eyes. Yet, there is even more to the Calceds' opinion of Fray Juan de la Cruz.

When all the orders were given by the Chapter to reduce or simply contain the growth of the Discalced, Fray Juan seemed to pay no heed. If he did not actively and personally countermand the orders of the Superior General and the Chapter, he certainly seemed to go along with the present acts of the Discalced. His silence was perceived as approval. His continued discussions with Madre Teresa implicated him in the revolt. He was behind all these difficulties, or so the Calced thought. This little friar who had once been one of them was now blatantly disobedient. And he was not simply disobeying a few minor rules. He was defying the highest authority in the order. Was this friar another Martin Luther determined to cause the Church so many problems? If so, he had to be stopped immediately. Obedience was a keystone of religious life. This Juan de la Cruz was breaking it down too openly. For the Calced, he was simply a disobedient rebel. In his stubborn pride, he would destroy the Order and perhaps lead the Spanish Church down the road to rebellion and even heresy. The Reform had to be stopped. A plan was drawn up. They would pounce on the leaders, toss them into prison, halt the growth of the reform, and, by these harsh measures, perhaps succeed in bringing the irksome revolutionaries to repent of their folly. They intended to execute their plan swiftly, before 1577 was finished.

The winter had already set in on the Avilan plain. The mountains in the distance were now covered in snow and seemed to be slowly spreading their white blanket toward the city of Avila. In their tiny hut, Fray Juan de la Cruz and his companion, Fray Germán de Santo Matía, tried to keep warm. The bitter winds and frost had already made the ground outside brittle and hard. They had both felt the piercing cold during that December day because they had to go to the monastery several times for Mass and other functions. Though the monastery was only a short walk away, Fray Juan felt the intense cold cut through him. Even the rather heavy rough habit did not protect him enough. The wind and cold bit his uncovered feet. The thin body shivered as he went. But now the two men were somewhat protected from the elements as they settled down for the night. The sun had gone down early on this December 2, 1577 as it does on any winter's night.

As they prayed together before retiring, they heard people coming toward their hut, their feet making a crunching sound as they hurried down the hill, almost running. What the two monks inside were soon to discover was that these people were Calced monks, some police and city people. They were coming to kidnap the two of them.

When they reached the door, they were not stopped by ceremony. They broke it open. As they rushed inside, there was a good deal of noise and confusion. Though neither of them resisted, the roughness with which they were handled bloodied the mouth of one of them. They were then dragged out of the building and quickly pushed up the hill to the Calced monastery on the city wall. The gang feared the noise would attract people and they wanted to hide their two prisoners as quickly as possible to avoid complications. The orders of Tostado, the Vicar General of the Order, were completed. These two were now arrested and safely in their hands.

Once in the monastery, the prisoners were forced to remove their rough habits of the reform and put on the more refined ones of the Calced friars. Then both were lashed twice and put in the monastic cells. However, the following morning, after Fray Juan had been freed to go to say Mass, he used this opportunity to escape back to the hut. He ran down the steep hill and into the hut to destroy some letters and documents which would have hurt the reform had they fallen into the hands of the Calced. But his captors quickly discovered his escape. They ran down the hill after him. He was almost finished by the time they arrived. He had bolted the door and when they came, he had just enough time to destroy the last papers as they pounded violently on the door.

Fearing he might escape again or that the people of the city would come to rescue him and Fray Germán, the Calced decided to transfer both of them. Fray Germán was sent to the Monastery of San Pablo de la Moraleja which is between Avila and Medina del Campo, while Fray Juan de la Cruz was taken to Toledo.

The very next day, the nuns of the Encarnación realized what had happened during the night. Several had heard the violent sounds coming from the direction of the huts, but they had not been able to figure out what was going on. Once they discovered the truth, no time was lost in telling the Madre about it. She was terribly upset. On December 4, 1577 she wrote a letter to King Felipe II of Spain who was then in Madrid.[1] In this letter she told him what had happened, along with some of the background. Then she said, "I am terribly saddened to see them in their (Calced) hands . . . and would feel better if they were prisoners of the Moors because they would then perhaps be treated better. And this monk (Fray Juan de la Cruz), so fine a servant of God, is so thin from all that he has suffered that I am afraid he will die."[2] This letter and others she wrote so furiously came to nothing. The king probably avoided the issue because disobedience in a religious community was often handled in this way. At any rate, while not forgotten, Fray Juan could not be effectively helped. What he was about to go through was his and his alone to bear. It was to be painful—even beyond imagining— but it was also to be THE most significant growth experience of his life.

The long trek to Toledo was not easy. The Calced did not want to take him there by the most direct route, fearing that if they passed through major towns and cities along the way, their prisoner might be recognized. Instead they went around, through the Sierra Guadarrama, as sleet and snow pounded down upon all of them. Fray Juan had to bear as well the jibes and taunts of his captors. The days seemed terribly long. The journey seemed so long, endless at times. When they finally approached the city, Fray Juan was exhausted, cold, and wet. To keep him from knowing exactly where he was, they blindfolded him and brought him into the city late at night, doubling back and forth upon their tracks.

The incredibly beautiful imperial city of Toledo, some seventy kilometers south of Madrid, rests on a hill above the Tagus river. Its ancient walls and cathedral dominate the skyline. Inside the walls, one is in the midst of a series of calm squares and steep, narrow walkways of cobblestone. The river that flows around the city protects it like a moat. In the winter, the cold stone walls of the majestic buildings hold off the cold sharp winds. In the summer, a stifling heat burns the ancient stones as the sun pounds the pavements. It is a mystic city, revealed as such in a painting by El Greco, who arrived there in 1577, the very year of the imprisonment of Fray Juan de la Cruz.

However, Fray Juan was not to see the beauty of this place. His view would be severely limited. The Toledo monastery of the Calced friars was one of the most striking in Spain. It was very large, housing some eighty monks quite comfortably. Yet within this rambling cloister Fray Juan was kept in a space hardly suitable even for storage.

He was thrown into a monastic cell, but shortly thereafter was transferred to another "cell," this one in fact only a closet for the adjoining guest room. The place was only six feet wide and ten feet long with no window and the solid wood door let in no light at all. The only illumination came from an opening about two inches wide high up in the wall which separated the room from a hallway. In order for Fray Juan to read, he had to stand on something and hold the book up to catch the faint rays of light that did manage to filter in. Even then it was very hard on his eyes, but in this way he managed to read his office.

The first minutes in this cell, as his eyes adjusted to the darkness, were terrifying. He stumbled across something on the floor. Gradually his eyes could see more in the darkness and with his fingers he found what was to be his bed: a couple of boards on the floor and an old blanket or two to protect himself just a bit from the wintry dampness of the cold stone floors and walls. A bucket sat in the corner. This was to be his toilet. But even before this pail was used, the room had a very unpleasant smell, for it was situated quite near to the monastery toilets. This dark and smelly place was to be his home for several more months. In fact it was to be a place of both physical and spiritual darkness, anguish, and pain.

The conditions in which they kept him wore him down slowly but surely. The food was minimal. Day after day, it was the same thing: a few scraps left over from the Carmelite table. As time went on he became weaker and more fatigued as well as paranoid. More and more he was certain that the monks were trying to kill him. This is seen in his reaction to the few sardines that he would receive occasionally as part of his meal. They were relatively rare and, as a result, heightened his suspicion that they were poisoned. His fear was so strong that each bit required a special effort to eat. And as he would eat these sardines he would attempt to distract himself by forgiving his imagined killers. The lack of proper food had weakened him considerably, yet despite this he was forced to undergo a very particular ceremony.

Every week on Fridays Fray Juan was dragged to the common dining room where he was given bread and water — his sole sustenance for that day. As the other monks ate their food on tables located around the walls of the large refectory, Fray Juan ate his bread kneeling on the hard, stone floor in the very center of the room. Once finished, the superior would begin to harangue him in the presence of all the others:

> You, Juan de la Cruz, are but a rebellious, stubborn man who desires nothing but your own fame and honor. In your hard-headedness you are destroying all that is good in Holy Mother Church and our own community of Carmel. At a time when our Mother Church is being beseiged by even more destructive forces from without, you, Juan, weaken it from within. You refuse to obey. Obedience, that faithful cornerstone of religious life, is treated by you as simply trash to be trampled under foot. The General Chapter of Piacenza ordered all you contemplatives not to establish new houses, not to wear a different habit, not to accept novices. But you persist in your own satanically inspired ways. Disregarding the commands of the General or the Chapter and even the orders of the representative of our Holy Father the Pope, you scandalize our holy order. You scandalize the people of our Holy Mother the Church. In all your stubbornness you weaken the faith of all believers. How can you maintain your satanic stance in the face of such horrors you are causing? Repent of your disobedience. We will forgive you and take you back into our very hearts. Work now with us to preserve the faith in this world

> that is so possessed by Satan and his cohorts. Repent of your
> disobedience. We only ask that you exercise your vow and the
> virtue of obedience and simply follow the commands of the
> Legate, your superiors and the General Chapter. Admit your
> disobedience and follow the orders of your Church and once
> again you will serve Holy Mother Church as She deserves to
> be served.

Friday after Friday (and at the beginning of his imprisonment, even more often), these and similar words rang out in
the echoing stone chamber of the dining room of the monastery. How strange and painful these words sounded to him,
and they were coming from good, sincere men: his fellow
Carmelites. What had he done that could cause them to regard him this way? Were they really talking about him? Was
he not simply following the orders of the higher authority,
the former Legate? Was the reform as evil as his superior
was now saying? The questions pressed upon him more and
more strongly as he heard these rebukes time and time
again.

While the final words of the Superior still rang in Fray
Juan's ears, all the monks would stand. One by one, they approached him as they chanted in unison the *Miserere*. First,
the prior and then each of the others would whip the bared
shoulders of the little revolutionary. The short, knotted tri-
ple rope they used bit into his flesh time after time. Those
who felt him most guilty put all the force they could into
their one blow. Others, who believed he was being treated
too harshly, felt the sting in their own hearts and bodies and
touched him as gently as they could. By the time he was led
back into his wintry hole in the wall, blood from his wounds
trickled from his back and shoulders.

As days lengthened into weeks and weeks into months,
conditions became worse. The monks promised to make him
superior of any house of theirs that he might want if only he

would obey them. They even promised to give him a gold crucifix. (How little they knew the man!) These bribes did not affect him, but their words of rebuke and correction did. "Maybe I am wrong," he thought. "Perhaps they are right. After all, I owe my obedience to my religious superiors and these men are my superiors. Am I to suffer all this simply to be sent to hell for my evil, recalcitrant ways? Am I to be separated from my God and my beloved Church for no reason at all? Am I serving the demons themselves?" He came to a point where he was no longer so sure of his position.

The weeks of imprisonment in this cold, foul-smelling and moldy cell with poor food took their toll. He kept losing weight. His appetite was failing and some days he simply could not eat at all. After a few months' imprisonment, poor food, little sleep, and lack of light so affected him that he began to suffer from dysentery. Some days he was not even allowed to empty his bucket. This intensified the horrid smell. Yet even this was not enough for his captors.

The monks persisted in their attempts to break his fidelity to the reform. They would talk outside his door saying how all the others of the reform had surrendered and returned to the Calced. Sometimes they would loudly suggest that this monk could be thrown into an empty well outside the city and no one would be the wiser. From their exaggerated statements made for his benefit, Fray Juan de la Cruz received greatly distorted ideas of what was actually happening. What reason was there for him to remain firm? Everyone else — even the leaders of the Discalced — seemed to have given up. Fray Juan was confused and doubted the reasonableness of going on anymore with this horrible thing. He had reached the point where he wished God would let him die. In fact, this is what he asked for himself.

Such release, however, was not to be his. Instead, in addition to all his physical pain and mental doubt, another element even more terrifying than the rest came. Up until now,

God had been the one steadfast part of his life. From his early years at the Medina del Campo Hospital de Las Bubas through his Carmelite days in the same city and in Salamanca, there had been for Fray Juan the realization of God's presence. True it had been wonderfully intensified during his days in Duruelo—those idyllic months when God seemed so real and so close. Even the joys of God he felt at the Encarnación seemed to pale in the light of Duruelo. The first months of imprisonment here in Toledo had been hard, but he could always pray and somehow know God to be present.

Now things had changed radically. He suffered the complete absence of God. It was not just a light, momentary absence, such as most believers know from experience. It was total. All his life, past and present, seemed to him to be wasted. He could no longer pray. The very thought of God made him sick, even physically sick. He felt abandoned in his degradation. He was terribly ill, with underclothes literally rotting away on his body. He who was so meticulous about personal cleanliness had not been able to wash for months. The summer heat was beginning: a stifling, unbearable, scorching heat. His closet cell was an oven. "Where is this cursed God? Why am I here? Why? Why?" Many years later Fray Juan de la Cruz would seem to be recalling this experience when he described the purifying flame of God and observed that ". . . a person suffers great deprivation and feels heavy afflictions in his spirit, which ordinarily overflow into the senses, for this flame is extremely oppressive. In this preparatory purgation the flame is not bright for a person, but dark . . . . It is not gentle, but afflictive. Even though it sometimes imparts the warmth of love, it does so with torment and pain. And it is not delightful, but it is consuming and contentious, making a person faint and suffer with self-knowledge. Thus it is not glorious for the soul, but rather makes it feel wretched and distressed in the spiritual light of self-knowledge which it bestows . . . . At this stage a person suffers from sharp trials in his intellect, severe dryness and distress in his will, and from the burdensome knowledge of his own miseries in his memory. In the substance of his soul he suffers abandonment, supreme poverty, dryness, cold and sometimes heat. He finds relief in nothing, nor is there a thought that consoles him, nor can he even raise his heart to God, so oppressed is he by this flame . . . . For when the soul suffers all these things jointly, it truly seems that God has become displeased with it and cruel."[3]

The spiritual pain and anguish simply cannot be narrated. He was crushed, destroyed. Unable to rise from the pit of his darkness, he languished alone, desperately alone, and cried out from the depths of his agonizing soul. All was for nothing. Then, to add to his troubles, he became filled with passion and desires. Some were things he had never imagined existed in him. Others were things he thought he had suppressed years ago. They kept coming back to his consciousness again and again. His sensitivity and imaginative ability heightened their visual intensity. All seemed to be dragging him, plunging him into darkness. He could do nothing but see it all, see himself and suffer it. For days and weeks, the physical and spiritual onslaught continued unrelentingly. He lived it out in crushing anguish. No one spoke to him and he spoke to no one. It was his ordeal to bear and to live. The exact days or weeks of this horrible trial are unknown, but by May, 1578 he had gone through the worst of it. He had been remade. The life of belief had reached a new stage; he had survived and grew. His experience became the basic pattern for his descriptions of the dark nights of the soul on its way to God.

In the spring of 1578, Fray Juan de la Cruz was given a new jailer, Fray Juan de Santa María. For months beforehand, this new guard had seen how badly the others had treated the prisoner. It was not very long before his close contact enabled him to see Fray Juan as he really was: kind, gentle, patient, even-tempered and faithful. Moreover, he saw how much the captive friar needed some change. He began by providing him with a clean new tunic to replace the old one he had been wearing since his imprisonment began. Then came a totally unexpected gift. While the other monks were at their daily siesta, he would unlock the door of Fray Juan's cell in order to let him roam about outside to get some light and fresh air. This was so appreciated by Fray Juan that he thanked the jailer profusely and gave him a small wooden crucifix with a bronze corpus which he had been wearing under his tunic near his heart. With the relationship developing so well, Fray Juan de la Cruz took the chance to ask if he could have some paper, pen, and ink in order to write down a few things. There was no hesitation in his new keeper's mind and soon Fray Juan got the materials he had wanted for so long.

During the many months he had been there, and particularly in the last few weeks, Fray Juan had kept himself busy in a special way. In an effort to keep his mind alert and hence keep himself alive, he had begun composing poems. His imagination allowed him to break out of his stultifying prison and roam the countryside. He remembered Segovia with its north and south winds blowing over the flat fields just above the silvery, noisy rush of the Eresma river that surrounded the cliffs on which the Alcazar is built. In his mind's eye, he travelled through luscious woodlands and grazing fields, touching and smelling all the beauty to be found there. He found lovers, passionate and full of desire and love for each other. He remembered the parts of scripture he loved so much: The Song of Songs, the various psalms. So, in this dark, dank jail, he now wrote down some of what he had worked out in his mind. He wrote the first thirty-one stanzas of the *Spiritual Canticle*, the *Song of the Soul that Rejoices in Knowing God through Faith*, the *Romance Poems on the Gospel "In Principio erat Verbum"*, and the *Romance on the*

Psalm "By the Waters of Babylon" (Ps. 136). He put them all down carefully on the paper he had been given and kept them close by. These contained the anguish and the beauty of who he was. They expressed the process that was making and had made him into who he was.

His suffering is captured as he writes: "By the rivers of Babylon I sat down weeping, there on the ground and remembering you, O Sion, whom I loved. In that sweet memory I wept even more . . . I died within myself for you and for you I revived, because the memory of you gave life and took it away. The strangers among whom I was captive rejoiced; they asked me to sing what I sang in Sion: Sing us a song from Sion, let's hear how it sounds. I said: How can I sing, in a strange land where I weep for Sion, sing of the happiness that I had there?"[4] The more famous *Spiritual Canticle* speaks of the desire for the Beloved whom he had come to know so deeply in his cell. Composing, recomposing these works in his mind kept him sane. Yet, his physical condition kept deteriorating. He was dying day by day. The summer heat was getting worse. He could hardly stand it. He still feared for his life. All the pain was still there, but it no longer controlled him. He had broken through and despite the continuing ordeal, he could live and grow.

Weak and tortured as he was, he still knew that something had to be done. Shortly before the feast of the Assumption, an unexpected visit caused him to decide. The cell door opened, and the Superior and two others came in. Fray Juan de la Cruz was hunched over on the floor. The Superior was terribly annoyed that Juan did not move, so he kicked him and said, "Why don't you rise when your superior comes in?"[5] With great effort, the tired little friar got up and excused himself because of his condition and because he had thought it was the jailer. At this point, Fray Juan bravely asked if he could say Mass the next day since it was the feast of the Assumption. The Superior's answer was rapid and stunning:

"Not in my lifetime you won't." With that, one of the two guests who was within said to the Superior, "Come Father, let's leave this hovel. It's too foul smelling."[6] The door slammed shut after them. The key turned in the lock. This unlocked his decision. It was definite now that escape was the only route left open to him.

When his new jailer had started easing his restrictions, Fray Juan began familiarizing himself with the section of the monastery he was in. He saw the adjoining room and the hallway, in which was an observation window with a small balcony from which one could see the city wall some twelve or so feet below and the Tagus river at the foot of the rocky cliffs. Now determined to leave this place, he looked about more carefully. One day he tried to measure the distance from the window to the wall. Taking some thread he had been given to sew up his tattered habit, he weighted it with a small rock and lowered it. This rough measurement let him see that, taking into account his own height, he might just be able to fall a short distance on to the wall. Escape seemed possible, but there were many problems. Would he wake someone and be caught if he tried to escape at night? How would he get the lock off the door? What would he use for a rope to climb down the window? Was it really possible? Fray Juan simply could not wait any longer. He had to chance it.

So he began planning the move. Each day when he went out, he would loosen the screws on the lock of his door, taking the screws out and replacing them. He did this until the final day which he had decided upon as the day of his escape. By now, they were loose enough so that he could simply push the door from the inside and the lock would fall off and he could get out. The monks were sleeping far enough away so that the falling lock would not arouse them. That day, he tore up his blankets into strips and sewed them together to form a rope. There was enough for about twelve feet; that seemed sufficient. He then took the handle of the candle lamp and attached it to one end. This hooklike device would hold his handmade rope to the balcony. Things were ready. His time outside during the siesta was spent once more setting up the details of the escape that night. When he was brought back to his cell, the jailer did not notice the loosened lock. Fray Juan was in the cell, somewhat apprehensive but determined to escape.

However, a new wrinkle developed and threatened to destroy his plans. Two visiting monks were given the room adjoining his cell to sleep in. It was a very hot night and they kept the door open to get more air. Furthermore, they had moved their beds to a place on the floor near the door. This would make it a bit cooler. Unfortunately, they did not retire early, but talked for some time. Meanwhile, Fray Juan struggled with his decision. Should he postpone his escape attempt? Perhaps another time would be better. But in the final analysis, he decided to go ahead. He waited and waited until around two A.M. when all seemed quiet. He pushed the door firmly, but quietly. The lock fell to the floor with what seemed like the burst of a canon to him. It woke the visitors. "Who's there?" they shouted. But Fray Juan remained still and quiet, his heart pounding within him as if it would break out. He held his breath. Would they get up? But they thought it was just some noise outside and went back to sleep. It was rather a dark night and so Fray Juan could only make out the shadows of the figures on the floor. He stepped carefully around them, with his make-shift rope in hand. Once out the door, he walked quickly to the balcony window. He attached the lamp handle to the wooden railing. Then he took his habit off and threw it onto the wall below. He started lowering himself down the rope. The wooden railing gave a little, but it held. By the time he reached the end of the rope, he realized that he would have to swing a little to fall directly onto the wall, which was less than two feet wide. Earlier work-men had loosened the top stones of the wall preparing to repair it the following day, inadvertently adding to the danger. If Fray Juan missed and fell on the other side of the wall, he would be killed by the fall on the jagged rock cliffs dropping into the Tagus river below. Knowing all this, yet determined to proceed, he let go and fell safely on the top of the wall. He put on his habit and went on.

Now he had to find a way off the wall and into the city. He must find the Discalced Carmelite nuns of Toledo! This was the only thought that now raced through his mind. They would help him. He was sure of that. He moved cautiously along the wall. The little light provided by the moon helped, but not much. Then he saw what he thought was an alleyway. He lowered himself down. However, he discovered to his dismay that it was in fact the garden of the nearby convent of nuns. If he were caught here, it would be a terrible scandal and he would be back in jail with even stricter surveillance. He frantically rushed around looking for a way out. The walls were too high and he was so weakened by the treatment he had received in prison that he could not seem to scale them. His heart beat more rapidly in panic. His breathing became heavier. He perspired profusely, his whole body racked in pain. Then, he must have had a sudden burst of energy and climbed out by the corner of the walls. He was now on top again, not exactly sure of how he had gotten there. He walked along the wall and then came down into what he was now certain was a street.

It was still dark but sunrise was not far off. A woman saw him and invited him into her house saying, "Fray, it is too dark to be outside. Come and spend the night with me." He walked on more quickly. Others who had been nearby ridiculed him and called after him. He began to run. He ran until he could run no longer. Where were the sisters? At last he was able to get directions to the convent. It was early when he arrived, so he sat to rest in an inner courtyard, invited by the owner, who was just coming home.

When he heard the convent bells ringing to summon the sisters to morning prayer, he went to the door and rang the monastery bell. When the portress came, Fray Juan de la Cruz, exhausted but happy to be in this haven, said, "Daughter, I am Fray Juan de la Cruz. I have just escaped from jail. Please tell the Superior that I am here."[7]

As soon as she heard, the Prioress, Madre Ana de los Angeles, rushed to the turnstile. Since one of the sisters who was ill had asked to go to confession, the Prioress who knew Fray Juan was an extraordinary confessor, admitted him to the cloister. After hearing the nun's confession, he spoke with the sisters. They were horrified at seeing his condition. Worn out, incredibly thin, pale and exhausted, covered with his oversized, dirty habit, he presented a pitiful sight. They gave him something to eat and listened to him.

Meanwhile, the Calced fathers had discovered his escape and sent people out to search for him. Two came to the convent seeking the keys for the Church next door to see if he was there. When they did not find him, they brought back the keys and tried indirectly to discover if the nuns knew of his whereabouts. The portress subtly avoided their questions, so the friars left without finding him.

However, the Prioress knew Fray Juan de la Cruz could not stay with them long. So she contacted a friend of the community, Don Pedro Gonzalez de Mendoza, who was a cathedral canon and administrator of the hospital of Santa Cruz there in Toledo. He came to the convent where they disguised Fray Juan in a cassock, then took him to the hospital. It was near the monastery from which he had just escaped; in fact, he could look out his window and see the monastery's balcony window.

Now Fray Juan was free to rest and pray. The great trial was over, but his life continued.

NOTES

1. *Obras Completas de Santa Teresa de Jesus*, Carta 208, p. 879.
2. *Obras Completas de Santa Teresa de Jesus*, Carta 208, p. 880.
3. *Living Flame of Love-B* I, 19-20, BAC, p. 838 (Kav., pp. 586-587).
4. *A Romance on the Psalm "By the Rivers of Babylon"* (Ps. 136), BAC, pp. 939-940. (Kav., pp. 733-734).
5. BNM, Ms. 12738, fol. 138.
6. Alonso de la Madre de Dios: *Vida, Virtudes*, BNM, Ms. 13460, fol. 126.
7. BNM, Ms. 12738, fol. 386.

V

Fray Juan de la Cruz' Leadership in Andalusia (1578–1588)

Once Fray Juan had rested and recovered somewhat from his ordeal, he was anxious to leave his Toledo hiding place and rejoin his community. Meanwhile, because of all the difficulties which they were having, the Discalced decided to hold yet another meeting at Almodovar del Campo on October 9, 1578. Though it lasted only a few days, the priors and important religious of the reform gathered there took a number of decisive steps.[1] Although some opposed the move because of the terribly delicate position they had been in since the arrival of the new Legate a year earlier, the "Chapter" went ahead and elected a "provincial." This could be and was construed as yet another rebellious act. (Once the Legate heard of it, he excommunicated all who had been at the Chapter.) They then proceeded to send Fray Nicolas de Jesús María and Fray Pedro de los Angeles to Rome to explain their position and to seek a separation of the Discalced from the Calced portion of the community. Finally they named Fray Juan de la Cruz superior of El Calvario, their monastery in Andalusia.

Fray Juan set out for El Calvario accompanied by two servants who were pressed on him by Don Pedro Gonzalez de Mendoza, who feared that such a long journey alone would be too strenuous for Fray Juan. On the way Fray Juan stopped to visit the Discaled nuns at Beas. The trip would not have been easy, even if he had been in excellent health. It was still warm and uncomfortable. The dryness of the summer had covered everything in the barren land with a gritty film of sand. He passed through those plains and finally arrived at the more fertile hills and valleys of Andalusia. By the time he reached Beas, he was so fatigued and emaciated that the nuns could hardly recognize him. They tried to cheer him up with a song, but even this did not do much to dispel the distance which his condition seemed to place between them. He seemed far away, and his features were gaunt and drawn.

For the first few days he was with them, Fray Juan was quiet and shy. As he rested, he began gradually to speak more freely and to be more relaxed in their company. However, he still did not impress some of the nuns very much. One day in talking with them about Madre Teresa, Fray Juan spoke of her as *hija mia*, my daughter. This reference to the Madre annoyed the superior, Madre Ana de Jesús. She really thought that this young monk was very insolent to talk about the great foundress as if she were simply an ignorant woman. Though she was later to be one of his most fervent disciples, his shyness and that one incident kept her from seeing the great spiritual potential that lay within him. We know this because she wrote to the Madre bemoaning the fact that she and her nuns had no one with whom to speak of spiritual things. In her answer Madre Teresa praised the qualities of Fray Juan so highly that Madre Ana was very surprised. She and her sisters had seen and heard only a rather common little priest. Now the superior paid more attention and came to see a deeply spiritual man. As time went on and the nuns got to know him better they would learn a great deal from him.

El Calvario

After a few days rest, Fray Juan continued his journey to El Calvario. It was a short distance, though the poor condition of the roads that wended their way through the hills and valleys and his own physical weakness made the trip difficult. The religious at El Calvario were waiting for him. Some were even afraid of the rigidity they believed he was sure to bring to their monastery as superior. He had been among the first to join the Discalced and his reputation from his days at Medina del Campo and Salamanca as a young student had been transmitted in the gossip of the religious grapevine. Now his imprisonment was bound to have made him even harder and more demanding they thought. The thirty friars awaited him with apprehension.

When Fray Juan de la Cruz arrived, they were surprised at the gentleness and kindness of this little friar who was to take the place of their superior while he was in Rome. This newly arrived friar was made for this isolated monastery in the Sierra Morenas. The area's hills and valleys, covered with fruit trees, olive groves and other vegetation, suited him perfectly. It was an ideal place to pray, rest and live out the life of a Discalced. It was such a contrast to the nine months of captivity in the closet cell that it was bound to rejuvenate Fray Juan.

The friars of El Calvario lived frugally. In fact, most of the time they ate weeds and other vegetation from the fields cooked with a bit of garlic and vinegar. If they had oil and vinegar, it was a most unusual day. They prayed together, as the rule required, in Choir, while the rest of the time they meditated privately in their cells. Fray Juan's cell was as simple as all the others. His bed was no more than a bundle of rosemary and brush woven together for a mattress. A small table and chair were the only other furniture in the room. It was his opinion that everyone had to be treated alike, whether they were superior or subject. All lived and worked together and when food was lacking, they would still gather in the refectory where Fray Juan would give the blessing, thanking God for having chosen them to suffer a little that day. Life in this monastery was a growing together in God.

Fray Juan would walk to Beas every Saturday to hear the confessions of the nuns, guide them on their spiritual journey and celebrate the Eucharist with them. These were days of great joy for the nuns and Fray Juan. Madre Magdalena del Espíritu Santo was one of the sisters who lived there at the time and she tells us how gentle and kind Fray Juan was. As he spoke, she says, "the other nuns also learned something of the great power which the holy father had with God and of the good effects which he produced in their souls; and also . . . his great mortification, and the detachment which he had from all that is not God, as well as his great gentleness and kindness."[2] In events like this we find the beginnings of the commentaries he wrote later on his poetry. The discussions with the nuns helped him to clarify his ideas and thus they became the stuff from which he created his masterful prose commentaries such as the *Spiritual Canticle* and the *Living Flame of Love*. It was through all this, moreover, that the sisters learned of his great gentleness, knowledge and deep humanity.

While at the convent, Fray Juan was never idle. In his free time he weeded the garden and cultivated flowers. He loved to be able to feel the earth, to be in contact with nature, which had inspired the poet in him so often. Each Monday, Fray Juan walked back to El Calvario still bearing within him the peace and restfulness which the Beas' stays gave him.

Spurred on by the questions and comments of the religious at Beas and particularly by their constant urging, Fray Juan de la Cruz began seriously writing commentaries on his poems. He wrote the *Ascent of Mount Carmel* and at the same time the first draft of the *Spiritual Canticle*. He also wrote the *Counsels* for the nuns at Beas. This short work consists of a series of admonitions meant to help the religious grow closer to God through their life as committed, consecrated Christians. The nuns greatly appreciated this work and also enjoyed receiving a sketch of Mount Carmel, which he drew for each of them. He was very successful in helping all who lived here, but he was also sad. He wanted to return to his native Castile, because he missed the people, the landscape with its fresh pines in the mountains and the burnt parchedness of the summer in the plains of the north. After two years of living in the South where he felt abandoned and the people were so different from the Spaniards with whom he had grown up, he was lonely and yearning to see his mother and brother once again. However, his return to Castile would be delayed for several more years. Right now he was needed in Baeza.

Baeza

Baeza was an important city in sixteenth-century Spain. With its 50,000 inhabitants and a very good university, it was a fine place for a new house of religious in Andalusia. Several leading university people from Baeza had heard of the Discalced and were doing all in their power to have these monks come to establish a monastery in their city. After some discussion, the Discalced decided that this would indeed be an excellent location for a house of studies, and they appointed Fray Juan de la Cruz as its founding rector.

Once he had discovered a place in which to establish a student residence, Fray Juan had to choose those who would be part of this new foundation. He chose three friars to go with him to establish the Colegio de San Basilio, the first house of studies of the Discalced. They set out for Baeza from El Calvario early on June 13, 1579. By nightfall they had finished the trip of some thirty miles on foot and were setting up the chapel for the opening Eucharist, which was to be celebrated the next morning, the Feast of the Holy Trinity, June 14, 1579.

The Colegio was situated not far from the University and very near to the Puerto de Ubeda. Today, the site of the Colegio is occupied by the Escuela de Artes Aplicados y Oficios

Artisticos with its large, modern building and garden. The Moorish walls of the city are not far away. The Colegio was situated like other Carmelite monasteries, on the fringes of the city. Though not in the heart of the city, it was in a *barrio* and hence very near it. Going from the Colegio to the University, Fray Juan could see the brown-tiled roof of the Cathedral through the arch of the Puerta de Ubeda, with its watch tower standing guard. The very narrow cobblestoned streets with stone houses crushing in on these small alleys blocked a panoramic view. They wound their way up and down slight inclines toward the city center. Once he had arrived at the immense Cathedral with the Fuente de Santa María at the side, he could see the massive stone buildings of the University and church. The short, square university building with ornate stone carvings around and above the doors reminds one of the immortal quality of medieval architecture. It was in this city of intellectuals and *beatas*, laywomen who lived alone in their houses and dressed as religious, that Fray Juan was to spend the next two years of his life.

His own life did not change much as Rector of Baeza. Poverty was still a key element of religious life for him. Though the monks lacked mattresses and pillows and some other things, Fray Juan was not willing to allow the bursar to go out and get the needed items from benefactors. He would say, " . . . what is it to be poor if we have everything we need?"[3] As if to prepare his fellow monks for living real poverty, he even refused to accept a gift of mattresses and other materials from someone at the university who had seen their poverty. He also continued to accent the life of recollection which he maintained should be at the heart of every Discalced Carmelite's life. For days on end the citizens of Baeza would not see the monks in the streets. They went out very seldom; usually even these rare periods outside were either to go to the University or to visit the sick. Once at a chapter of faults the provincial rebuked Fray Juan for not going out more often to visit the rich and influential lay people. He prostrated himself before the provincial and said that if he used this time to ask God to move these people to give what was necessary and they did it, would not that be good enough? There was silence. Fray Juan had made his point. It was his view that prevailed. He was always the first in giving the right example and in this way he set the tone for life in the new Colegio.

Fray Juan's days were filled with the ordinary. He cleaned the house, arranged the chapel, did repairs as they were needed. He did not use his position as superior to get out of the day to day work which was required in this community. Fray Juan de la Cruz always saw himself as one of the many brothers who lived and worked together. In his spare moments, he would continue his work on the *Ascent* and the *Canticle*. He prayed and read the scriptures. Often he slept only two or three hours nightly and spent the remaining hours praying in the chapel. When he did this, he sometimes would be found with his head on his cape on the chapel floor. There he rested with his God.

The liturgy was very important to him. The devotion to common prayer that he had always had grew deeper. Not only was he extremely fastidious about the cleanliness of the altar and vestments, but he became creative on special days. For example, at Christmas, he would have plays performed by the monks. Monks would be dispersed throughout the monastery to act as the innkeepers of Bethlehem, while he and others would take the roles of the holy family. Stopping at each group of monks, he would speak of the wonders of Christmas. His face shone. His features came alive as he spoke of this mystery. His eyes brightened and were filled with joy. Doña María de Paz, a beata of Baeza, spoke of seeing him at different seasons and how his whole body, but especially his face, seemed to reveal the mood of the season.[4] Fray Juan was like all human beings whose heart can be read in their physical appearance, if one looks carefully.

He was a man of striking honesty for his time. One day, someone came to the Colegio with some stipends for masses which had to be said on particular dates. Since all the monks already were occupied those days, Fray Juan ordered that the stipends should not be accepted. One of his assistants said that perhaps, since one day more or less was not really important and since they needed the money, they could nonetheless accept the stipends and say the masses at a later date. However, Fray Juan firmly maintained that they were to be truthful first and foremost and leave their needs to God.

A striking characteristic of Fray Juan de la Cruz is described by Fray Juan de Santa Eufemia.[5] According to the constitution of the order, the superior was to visit the cells of the monks to make sure they were not disobeying the rules. Fray Juan would do this, but as he went along he would rattle his rosary, thereby making enough noise to warn them he was coming. He was never out to catch someone doing something wrong. He saw the rule and its fulfillment as a way of helping others to live out their religious lives more fully. This human, considerate quality is also demonstrated by Fray Juan's conduct during recreation periods. After supper the monks would go to a common room to listen to Fray Juan and to relax a little. His conversations were so fascinating that the monks always left that room laughing or rested. Whether he spoke of ordinary things or spiritual thngs, his hearers were always happy when they departed. In fact, the monks looked forward to these evening encounters so much that those who had to serve often skipped their meals in order to hear him and be with him. Only a totally human and compassionate man could command such love and devotion.

Fray Juan's compassion came to the fore once again in his concern and care for the sick. 1580 was the year of the *catarro universal*, an influenza epidemic which hit the whole of Spain. Whole families would often be ill at the same time. One such case was the family of one of the monks at San Basilio. So Fray Juan went with him to visit and found all the members of the family spread out in different rooms. Fray Juan spoke with them and comforted them as well as he could. Back at the Colegio, the rooms were filled with his own sick monks, as well as some nine others who had been brought there from El Calvario to be treated. Fray Juan changed beds, washed the patients, fed them and sometimes even cooked for them. His gentleness and deep concern made him loved even more.

The influenza also struck Medina del Campo. Juan's mother, who had been living there, was taken seriously ill and died shortly afterward. Out of respect for Fray Juan and because she herself had been so close to the nuns, the Discalced nuns had her buried in their own cemetery. Only his brother remained and he would be a great joy to Fray Juan de la Cruz in the closing years of the little friar's own life.

While Rector at the Colegio, a good deal of Fray Juan de la Cruz's time was occupied with spiritual guidance. Students, some of the beatas and ordinary people were among those who sought him out as they made their journey to God. Some of the teachers at the University also came almost daily to reflect with Fray Juan on scripture, as well as to receive advice about their own spiritual growth. Among them were Dr. Ojeda, Maestro Sepulveda, Drs. Becerra and Carleval as well as Padre Nuñez Marcelo. All were amazed at the exactitude and newness of his interpretation of certain scriptural passages. What they gradually came to realize was that Fray Juan saw scripture in creative ways because he himself approached it as the source of his own daily life. It was not simply a question of finding a pertinent text for any given event. Rather, Fray Juan de la Cruz lived each moment of his life so fully that he could then read the Bible and constantly see the newness it offered. Scripture was being incarnated daily because Fray Juan knew life.

In Baeza, Fray Juan surprised everyone who knew him by

his intense love of nature. He would speak eloquently of the simplest flower in the field. A Spanish sky filled with hundreds of stars would send him into an ongoing praise of the God who had given humanity such beauty. He would often take someone out to the fields and, after having prayed alone, Fray Juan would rejoin him and begin talking about the beauty that surrounded them and the God whom it spoke of.

Yet, despite all the joys that the countryside offered him and all the activity and prayer that kept him more than occupied, Fray Juan de la Cruz was still sad. He openly speaks about it in a letter to Madre Catalina de Jesús dated July 6, 1581: "Although I know not where you are, I want to write these lines trusting that our *Madre* will send them on to you if you are not with her. And if it is so—that you are not with her —be consoled with the thought that you are not as abandoned and alone as I am down here. For after that whale swallowed me up [a biblical allusion to his imprisonment in Toledo] and vomited me out upon this alien port, I have never merited to see her again nor the saints up there. God has done well, for after all, abandonment is a file and the endurance of darkness leads to great light."[6] The letter ends abruptly as if he had been totally exhausted by the thoughts of loneliness and darkness he had put down on paper. The night had not finished its work in Toledo. The whole situation must have been almost intolerable, for he sought help from Madre Teresa to get him back north to Castile. Nonetheless, he would have to wait some seven more years before he could go to live in his native region where he always felt more at ease. For now he continued in Baeza. He helped everyone without distinction and demanded that laypeople who sought any assistance from the monks always find an open door. Though he and the others would be exhausted and constantly sought out by the people, their role was to receive and help them. Fray Juan knew that as believers in Jesus their lives were to be fully involved in the world in which they lived. His cross was the path to life—to learn to let go is the message of suffering. Baeza was his life NOW and he lived it to the full.

After much negotiating, the Discalced finally got what they had sought for so long. On June 22, 1580, Pope Gregory XIII issued a Brief authorizing the separation of the Discalced Carmelites from the Calced. But it was only in November that Padre Maestro Fray Juan de las Cuevas, a Dominican, was named executor of the Brief. He called the first legal Chapter of the Discalced, which took place amidst much splendor and pomp on March 3, 1581. The following day Fray Juan de la Cruz was elected one of the Definitors of the community along with Padres Nicolás de Jesús María (Doria), Antonio de Jesús and Gabriel de la Asunción. Though many of the members of the Chapter wanted either Fray Juan de la Cruz or Fray Antonio de Jesús as Provincial, Padre Jeronimo de la Madre de Dios (Gracian) was elected. The executor, Padre de la Cuevas, favored Gracian for several reasons. Fray Juan's election as Definitor began a period of intense administrative and spiritual activity that would end only a few months before his death ten years later.

During his stay at Baeza Fray Juan travelled a good deal. He continued to be the confessor and director of the nuns at Beas. However, since he could now go only once or twice a month, he would stay a little longer than the one or two days he was accustomed to when he was in El Calvario. He went to Caravaca for the election of the Prioress in June, 1581. By November he was in Avila trying to convince Teresa to personally establish a convent in Granada. Instead, she sent him with some sisters and appointed Madre Ana De Jesús of Beas as superior. From December 8 until January 15, 1582 Fray Juan waited in Beas for the license to establish the convent in Granada. Things moved slowly. When he and the sisters could wait no longer, they set off for Granada and stopped

three miles outside the city. The trip had been terribly difficult. Rain had turned roads into pools of mud, and many
roads simply were not passable. At Albolete on January 19,
1582 the Vicar Provincial told them the Archbishop still had
not given permission for them to set up the convent. Furthermore, the house they were to have was suddenly no longer
available. Despite all this they decided to go ahead and arrived
on January 20 at the house of a rich woman who had promised
to help them: Señora Ana de Peñalosa, who was to be the great
friend and benefactress of Fray Juan de la Cruz in Segovia.
Fray Juan then went to the monastery of Los Martires to live
with the friars until the sisters were finally settled. It was to be a
longer and more official stay than he had planned.

Los Martires

The striking setting of Los Martires fit Fray Juan's own personality very well. To reach the monastery one had to make
an exhausting climb up the steep hill on the top of which sits
the Alhambra, an ancient Moorish palace. Los Martires lies a
little lower than the Alhambra and to its right. Between these
monuments to the two great religious traditions of Andalusia
lies a small canyon, filled now with trees. The monastery was
simple and small. It was built in a garden which originally
held conical pits which served as dungeons for the Christians
during the Moorish occupation of Spain. When the friars had
taken over a few years earlier, they had planted vines, bushes,
and trees. Their pond was supplied with water from the Alhambra. It flowed in, as it does today by means of an aqueduct. From the precipice on which it was built, the monastery
overlooked the plains spreading southward far below. At the
bottom of the steep incline were a few houses, but the main
part of the city of Granada could not be seen. It lay on the
other side of the Alhambra. However, opposite the precipice
with its view of the plains, one could see the foothills and the
snow-capped mountains of the Sierra Nevadas to the north.

The infinity symbolized by these mountains and the spreading plains below, as well as the beauty of the vegetation and man-made edifices, struck Fray Juan. Here was God's creation in all its variety and wonder. The friars of Los Martires decided to make use of the prerogative granted to houses of the Discalced in the new constitutions that allowed them to elect as their prior anyone in the province, even though he might already be a superior in some other house. They elected Fray Juan de la Cruz to be their superior in March, 1582. So began the six years of his residency in Granada although the last three years of his term involved so much travelling that he can hardly be said to have actually resided in Granada during that period.

It was during the years at Granada that the personality of Fray Juan flourished. Granada, the city of incredible beauty, had become for him the spring rain that makes the trees and flowers bloom. His ever present love for the sick, his concern for the poor, and his love of solitude were all clearly seen. He himself might be poor and suffering, but that mattered little as long as he could alleviate the pain of others.

One day while he was prior in Granada, one of the brothers fell ill. Fray Juan was very concerned and called the doctor. The doctor told Juan that there was nothing that could be done to cure him though there was some medicine that would alleviate some of his pain. However, he went on to say how costly this medicine was. With not a moment's hesitation, Fray Juan asked for the prescription and sent off to have it filled immediately. This is only one example of his real care of those who were ill.

Anytime the friars were sick, Fray Juan de la Cruz would visit them and stay with them. He would speak with them or spend hours by their bedsides in silence, holding their hands, wiping their feverish brows, feeding them. He would talk about something that would help them to relax and rest. Sometimes he spoke of God and the love God showered on all human beings. Or he would talk about the community or the weather or the beauty of nature. He adapted his conversation to the needs of the individual. What was important was that the sick person be consoled. But Fray Juan did not find these conversations dull or boring. If he spoke about things that helped another, it was always something that interested him too. He never put on airs. His sincerity was apparent to all observers. One could be sure that whatever Fray Juan said or did, it came from the depths of who he was.

When his duties as Vicar Provincial obliged Fray Juan to visit several Carmelite houses, he would always ask to see the sick as soon as he arrived. Once in the infirmary, it was as if he were home, as if he were sixteen again in the hospital at Medina del Campo. He would visit with them and see how they were. If they had not been eating, he would name different kinds of food they might want. Once he knew what they would like to eat, he himself often went out and prepared it and returned to feed them himself. Whether the patient was old or young, educated or not, he was their loving brother. The tenderness of Fray Juan was truly remarkable and it was not unnoticed by those who met him.

His special qualities were brought to the fore during 1584 when there was a famine in Andalusia. Crops had failed. Food was very scarce. Many people came into the city from the country in search of food and help. Los Martires received many callers looking for food and assistance. Fray Juan and the others knew their own supply was limited. Nonetheless, Fray Juan had no hesitation in giving food to all who came. No one was refused. In fact, there were some rather highly placed families who were lacking food, and Fray Juan discreetly sent them some. That way they did not lose face by coming to the monastery to beg. Fray Juan constantly showed his love and sensitivity to all kinds of people in whatever situation they were in.

Fray Juan responded generously, giving freely of his time and efforts. Whether he had been at prayer or work, if someone called upon him, he left it all to come to them. God, for him, was never absent and so whatever he did, Fray Juan knew it was always in that Presence. It was because of this deep consciousness of God's presence that he was able to bring people to hope even when they wanted to doubt everything. Fray Juan would show these discouraged people the positive aspects of their lives and thus help them to go on. In dealing with people afflicted by scruples and tempted to despair, he was the perfect example of kindness, mercy, and gentleness. It was this deep understanding of people that enabled him to be confessor of many, many people in Granada. Priests, religious, laymen and laywomen, rich and poor came to him. They came because they knew he was one who understood and who could therefore be the sacrament of God's presence for them.

In sixteenth-century Spain, the prior of a monastery had a very high social standing. However, Fray Juan was not one to be impressed by such class distinctions or social games. One day while he was helping some workers on the monastery grounds, an important religious superior came to visit him. The porter went out to find Fray Juan to tell him. The other brothers and workers who were impressed by the eminence of their visitor suggested that he go in and clean up. However, Fray Juan was not about to do anything special. He simply had the porter bring the visitor to him as he was and where he was. Another time, a superior from a different religious community came to visit and said to Fray Juan: "My dear Father, since you keep yourself here in the monastery and we do not see you in the city, we would think you were the son of some worker." Fray Juan answered him with a touch of annoyance saying: "Oh I am not so highly placed a person. I am simply the son of a weaver."[7] His visitor understood.

When Fray Juan spoke, people were impressed because he was so authentic. Fray Martin de San José said: ". . . neither before nor since, either in a religious community or outside it, have I heard a person who could treat of God so beautifully."[8] His words were his own, nurtured by his prayer and by his interaction with his fellow human beings. While his studies surely provided him with a great deal, the warmth of his words came from an intimate knowledge of the God of whom he spoke. Listening to him, one always became calm and serene. It seemed as if all difficulties disappeared. People were ready to go on living with enthusiasm. Whether it was a homily he gave, a short talk or simply a conversation, the effect on his hearers was the same: they were filled with peace and love. Fray Juan Evangelista, who had been a novice under Fray Juan and who was his companion for the last years of his life, said that when Fray Juan would speak to them in recreation, he would most often speak of God, but never in a dry, overly serious way. He would speak of Him in such a way that the brothers would laugh and go out filled with great joy.[9] Fray Juan, like the psalmists of biblical times, was an intimate friend of God. God was so real, so close, that he could be part of one's sense of humor.

Fray Juan de la Cruz was certainly not a staid, serious, unapproachable man. Yet, in all this it must be remembered that he still loved solitude. It provided him with a sense of freedom. His mind and heart could wander with God over all the things of beauty and life. When he was alone he would read the scriptures and let God's word sink deeply into his heart. Solitude was not just a chance to get away from it all. It made it possible for him to love God and his brothers more fully. Solitude was to be with God and in this way to become more God-like. To reach this point of true solitude, the world and particularly people became very special to him. He urged his brothers to solitude. He and they had chosen a life of recollection and withdrawal from the fantasies of society. He knew he had not withdrawn from the world, only from the games of men who set up classes and divisions. Solitude with his God brought Fray Juan to see the beauty of the world and the equality of human beings more clearly. His father and mother had suffered because of the rules of society. His brother Francisco was considered by many a humiliating creature because of his poverty. For Fray Juan, solitude taught him the truth about the world. With this insight, he could become more deeply human and simple.

His cell in Granada, as in the other convents he had lived in, was the poorest of all. It was small and narrow with only a small table and bench, a bed with straw for a mattress and a small painted crucifix on the wall. Only a Bible and a *Flos Sanctorum* adorned the table. His habit was old and whenever he needed something, he would go to the storeroom and choose the oldest and most worn thing, saying that this was enough for him.

His days in Granada were full. He would visit the nuns of the monastery below Los Martires. There he would sit on one side of the grate in the speaking parlor while the nuns would gather on the other side to listen to him speak for about an hour. He constantly told them to let go of all that was not God. He guided them, listened, explained and helped all to grow in God. He did this as well with the nuns at Beas whom he still visited regularly though not as often as he had done when he was in El Calvario.

On one of these trips to Beas a woman holding a small baby approached him and said that the child was his and he should provide for its keep. Fray Juan asked about the mother and was told she was a fine woman who had never left Granada. Then he asked how old the child was. On learning the child was a year old, Fray Juan said, "Let us praise God for this miracle, because I've been in Granada for less than a year and I've never been here before."[10] He chuckled all the way to Beas and when he arrived he could hardly wait to tell the superior about what happened. And he laughed as he told her the story.

On May 1, 1583 Fray Juan was in Almodovar del Campo for the second chapter of the reform. The Provincial, Padre Gracian, urged a more active role for the community. Fray

Juan de la Cruz opposed this and argued that the Discalced were primarily a group of contemplatives. Any activity which took them away from this should be avoided. However, he did say that some apostolic work was a part of their lives as religious. He simply wished to avoid having the contemplative dimension put in second place. After his trip to Almodovar, when he was not visiting Beas or teaching the nuns at Granada, Fray Juan would write. In the same year as the famine, 1584, Fray Juan wrote the first draft of the *Canticle*, the poem the *Living Flame*, and perhaps even the commentary.[11] Madre Ana de Jesús heard Fray Juan talk about his poem the *Canticle* and urged him to write down his commentaries. After some persistence, she finally succeeded in getting him to write down his reflections in an orderly fashion. The process was rather simple. After speaking with the nuns, he would return to his monastery and think about some of the themes they had spoken about. Then he would write these thoughts down. This way he was able to complete the *Canticle* (and at the same time the *Ascent* and the *Dark Night*) and then, in about fourteen days, the commentary of the *Living Flame of Love*. The Living Flame commentary was done at the insistence of Ana de Peñalosa. The period at Granada was the most productive literary-wise of all his years. His major works were complete and only some revisions of the second writing of the *Canticle* and the *Living Flame* were yet to be done. These would wait until toward the end of his life.

In 1585 a new period of administration and travel began. In February he travelled the eighty-four miles between Granada and Málaga to establish the convent of Discalced nuns in this seashore city. The city with the mountains forming a backdrop to the city thoroughly enticed Fray Juan. His love for this convent was due at least in part to its idyllic setting. By the 10th of May, Fray Juan was in Lisbon for the General Chapter.

While he was in Lisbon, he was invited several times to go to see a Madre María de la Visitación, Prioress of the Dominican convent of the Anunciada. Everyone had heard of her not only in Portugal but in Spain. She experienced raptures and ecstacies and had the stigmata as well. Many prominent people — theologians and priests among them — had seen her and been impressed. When he returned to Granada, after being elected Second Definitor and Vicar Provincial, he was asked if he had seen her. He responded, "I did not see the nun, nor did I desire to do so because I would not think much of my own faith if I thought it would grow one iota by seeing her."[12] Fray Juan's faith was not built upon ecstacies and visions, but purely upon trust in God. As it turned out, the nun was later shown to be a fraud.

As Vicar Provincial Fray Juan was obliged to travel throughout the region of Andalusia a good deal. On his trips he would sing psalms and hymns, read scripture passages, and pray. He found the beautiful rugged landscape of southern Spain lent itself to constant prayer. Whenever he was on a trip, if he had to sleep over, he would sleep on a blanket on the floor. He normally took little sleep and used the time he saved to pray and reflect. His new life-style would provide him with ample material for this reflection.

Between 1585 and June of 1588, Fray Juan seemed to be on the road continually. In the fall of 1585 he attended the adjournment of the Chapter in Pastrana. Travelling back to Granada, he presided over the reelection of Ana de Jesús as Prioress in January, 1586. In 1586 he founded a priory at Cordoba, visited Sevilla, Ecija, and Cordoba, and fell ill at Guadalcazar. At Cordoba, he was working in a cell of the monastery when a stone wall on which laborers were working fell on that section of the monastery. Friars and men worked frantically to remove the rubble. They were afraid Fray Juan had been crushed to death. However, when they did find him, he was crouched in the corner and laughingly said the Virgin Mary had protected him with her cape. A stone statue of the Virgin stood above him in the corner he had rushed to upon hearing the falling wall.

His illness at Guadalcazar, not far from Cordoba, revealed

part of Fray Juan's ascetical practices. When a monk came to apply some oil to relieve a pain in his side caused by an abcessed lung, he discovered a chain around Fray Juan's waist that had been worn so long that it was partly imbedded in the flesh. With Fray Juan's consent it was removed. No more is heard after this about such practices.

Once he recovered sufficiently Fray Juan continued his journeys. The rest of 1586 found him in Madrid, La Manchuela, Granada, Caravaca, Beas, Bujalance and Madrid again in December. Another year of travel was his lot in 1587 but in June 1588 at the first Chapter-General of the Discalced at Madrid Fray Juan was appointed First Definitor and Counselor General and on August 10 he assumed the position of Prior in Segovia. He was back in his Castile, but his stay was to be short and fraught with problems.

NOTES

1. Though most scholars maintain that Fray Juan de la Cruz attended this meeting, the more recent study of P. Hipolito de la Sagrada Familia shows that he was not present: "La 'Vida de S. Juan de la Cruz' por el Padre Crisogono de Jesus. Reparos criticos" in *Monte Carmelo* 77 (1969), pp. 8-9.

2. E.A. Peers, ed., *The Complete Works of St. John of the Cross*, Vol. III, (Wheathampstead-Hartfordshire: Anthony Clarke, 1974), p. 297.

3. BMC vol. 14, p. 62 (BNM Ms. 12738, fol. 217).

4. BMC vol. 14, p. 45 (BNM Ms. 12738, fol. 184). The same thing is said by Martin de la Asunción BMC vol. 14, p. 88 (BNM Ms. 12738, ca. fol. 132).

5. BMC vol. 14, p. 28 (BNM Ms 12738, ca. fol. 144).

6. Letter no. 1, BAC, p. 971 (Kav., p. 685).

7. BMC vol. 14, p. 384 (BNM Ms 19404, ca. fol. 176).

8. BMC vol. 13, p. 378 (BNM Ms. 12738, ca. fol. 855).

9. BMC vol. 13, p. 386 (BNM Ms. 12738, ca. fol. 559).

10. BNM 12738, fol. 985.

11. Eulogio de la Virgen del Carmen, *San Juan de la Cruz y sus escritos* (teologia y Siglo XX), (Madrid: Ediciones Cristiandad, 1969), pp. 246-247.

12. BMC vol. 14, p. 13 (BNM Ms. 12738, ca. fol. 127).

VI

The Final Years, Segovia and Ubeda (1588–1591)

After years of waiting and hoping, Fray Juan de la Cruz grew resigned to his Andalusian exile and began the final three years of his life in glory. When he attended the General Chapter in Madrid on June 19, 1588, he was elected First Definitor. This meant that he was in charge of the Consulta whenever Padre Doria, the Vicar-General, was absent. (In fact, this meant that in the first year, Fray Juan presided over the Consulta almost the whole time.) The Vicar-General was very happy with this arrangement since up to now he and Fray Juan had been of the same mind and he felt he could continue to count on this support. Doria could not countenance opposition to his own ideas, yet he should have known that eventually something would come up that would cause Fray Juan to take a position different from his own. Initially, however, Fray Juan found himself in a rather pleasant situation.

Besides being elected to this position on the Consulta, Fray Juan was also appointed Prior of Segovia. Ironically, the monastery there had been founded on May 3, 1586, through the instigation of Fray Juan himself when he was still in Granada. Doña Ana de Mercado y Peñalosa, who had helped the Discalced nuns when they first arrived in Granada, was fulfilling the will of her husband who had asked that either a hospital or a monastery be built in his native city of Segovia. Fray Juan encouraged her to build a monastery for the Discalced. By the time Fray Juan arrived, the Discalced had already been living in the former Trinitarian monastery for two years.

Renovated and restored, the monastery still stands just outside the city across the Eresma river. Facing the monastery and towering above it on the cliffs which drop sharply to the river is the royal palace, the Alcazar, rising like a Spanish galleon from the valley below. In back of the monastery are small gardens reaching up to a natural wall. Within this rocky surrounding are caves from which one can see the beautiful panorama of this old Roman city.

Originally, the monastery was very close to the river. Hence the place was very damp and it was decided to build living quarters further up the hill away from the gurgling water. When Fray Juan arrived in August, 1588, he saw to the beginning of the new monastic construction. But he did not just oversee the work; he designed a special aqueduct system and then actually worked with the laborers. He loved the manual work, much of which was done in the winter. The snow and cold did not stop him. Barefooted, his worn habit all that protected him from the cold winds, he gathered stones from nearby and carried them to where the masons would place them. Despite the weather he enjoyed being with the men and seeing the monastery develop. There was something about this work that suited him. In addition, he was able to pray during this time. He was more and more able to find God among these fellow workers as well as in his fellow monks.

During his prayer, his work, and his conversation, the world of God and the world of human beings became one for Fray Juan. Everything became a symbol of God's presence and the very thought of God made creatures and creation more present to him as well. He wrote, "And here lies the remarkable delight of this awakening: the soul knows creatures through God and not God through creatures."[1] Union with God brought him to love and see more fully the world in which he lived. It rooted him in this life, in this creation of his God.

His life was extremely active in the Segovian period. During the first year, with the absence of the Vicar-General, Fray Juan had to handle the multitude of administrative details connected with his role as superior of the order. The construction was continuing. He, moreover, gave spiritual advice to some of the nuns in Beas and Granada by correspondence. In the meantime Doña Ana de Mercado y Peñalosa had moved to Segovia. This meant that she and her niece would seek spiritual direction from Fray Juan at the monastery itself. And frequently he would go to their home and visit them as well. While there he would speak with the servants about their daily routine as well as about God and their path to Him. Many people would go to the monastery to seek him out. Don Juan de Orozco y Covarrubias, archdeacon of Cuéllar and Canon of Segovia, and Diego Muñoz de Godoy, Canon of Segovia, both knew Fray Juan and were always impressed by their visits to him. However, it was Dr. Villegas, the Canon-Penitentiary, whom most witnesses remark on in a special way.

In addition to his duties as Penitentiary, Dr. Villegas was also the confessor of the Discalced nuns in Segovia. It was no doubt because of his deep and stable spiritual life that he had been asked to perform this ministry. Because Fray Juan was so involved with the nuns and the administration of the community, his advice on such an appointment was always closely heeded. It is no wonder that Dr. Villegas visited him often. The two would walk together into the garden at the back of the monastery. Then they would sit on the ground together and talk. For four or five hours at a time they would speak about their lives and God's presence with them. Their friendship grew stronger and stronger as time went on, and Fray Juan thoroughly enjoyed these serene hours with Dr. Villegas. He liked only one other person's company as much.

Fray Juan's beloved brother Francisco also came to visit him. Now that Juan was in Castile once more, it was easier for the two brothers to see each other. Francisco would come, expecting to stay a day or two, but Fray Juan would urge him to stay another and yet another, until finally Francisco would simply have to get back to his family. Sometimes weeks had elapsed. Though Fray Juan was a superior, and hence had a great social standing, he was not about to hide his poor brother from the others. He would introduce Francisco to high and low alike as his " . . . brother, who is my greatest treasure on earth." Fray Juan never attempted to change his brother or make him more presentable socially. He felt that neither poverty nor ignorance makes any person less a human being than another.

During one of these visits, Fray Juan told Francisco of a unique experience. It seems that one day as Fray Juan was in prayer before a picture of Christ carrying the cross,[2] he heard an interior voice calling his name. This happened several times. Finally, he said inwardly, "Here I am." And the voice said, "What reward would you like to have from me for all you have done and all you have suffered?" Fray Juan de la Cruz responded, "To suffer and to be looked down upon." After having told Francisco this Fray Juan added: "So, if you see me with trials, don't worry Francisco, for these are what I have asked for from the Lord. He will help me to live them out and so to grow more deeply." Those times of trials would indeed come, but not immediately.

Fray Juan was busy, but he cultivated his sense of poverty and solitude so that he could effectively minister to others. As had been his usual practice, when he arrived in Segovia, Fray Juan chose the most obscure cell there was. It was again a very small room under the staircase adjoining the choir section of the chapel. A couple of boards formed the bed and another was attached to the wall. This was his writing table. The cell was as plain and simple as his food. He ate little, fasting according to the rule. When something special was sent into the monastery, he would give it to the monks while he ate the normal fare. His prayer times became increasingly more frequent. Special moments of prayer were most often found at night while the others slept. Like many other creative people, Fray Juan did not need much sleep; two or three hours a night sufficed. The rest of the time, he might be found in the chapel kneeling with his arms outstretched or looking out a monastery window at the clear, star-filled Segovian sky, enthralled by the beauty God had showered on this world. He would also go up to one of the small caves in the cliffs behind the monastery when he had some spare time, and there he would pray in quiet as he watched the birds fly in and out of the crevices of the rocks. These times not only strengthened him; they were very normal parts of the daily rhythm of his life. There was a natural flow to his life and these times were all part of it. The busy yet calm and prayerful times were important preparations for what was to come.

In 1590 at an extraordinary Chapter, Fray Juan disagreed with some ideas Padre Doria put before the meeting. The most contentious issue concerned the Discalced nuns. While Doria wanted them to be governed by the Consulta (a procedure that would have complicated their affairs), the nuns wanted to be governed by one person appointed by the Consulta. Fray Juan took their side, and this annoyed the Vicar-General so much so that Doria began to plan how he could be rid of him.

His opportunity came at the General Chapter held on June 1, 1591, when Fray Juan once more opposed the General's excess in legislating policy for the community. Again he took up the position of the nuns and also defended Padre Gracian, whom Fray Juan felt was being treated unfairly. Though some agreed with him privately, publicly they sided with the Vicar-General. Fray Juan was not elected to the Consulta and was removed from his post as Prior of Segovia. During the Chapter, Fray Juan offered himself as one of the twelve Discalced who were needed to help their province in Mexico. The offer was accepted, but later that decision was reversed.

After many years in important administrative positions, the little friar was once again an ordinary monk. He did not mind this very much, although he was concerned about the direction the order was taking. However, he was starting a new ministry, and he went first to La Peñuela to await his departure for the New World. He was not feeling well when he set out, and the long trip had exhausted him. Nonetheless, he began at this time to rework some of his writings. The solitude and quiet of this Andalusian retreat was conducive to this work, and he produced the second edition of the *Canticle* and the *Flame* during this period. This activity was in addition to the normal round of duties of a monk living in a monastery. We get an insight into how he felt about his life at this time from a letter he wrote to Doña Ana de Mercado y Peñalosa on August 19, 1591:

> I mentioned in the other letter how I desire to remain in this desert of La Peñuela, where I arrived about nine days ago and which is about six leagues north of Baeza. I like it very much, glory to God, and I am well. The vastness of the desert is a great help to the soul and body, although the soul fares very poorly. The Lord must be desiring that it have its spiritual desert. Well and good, for His Majesty already knows what we are of ourselves. I don't know how long this will last, for Padre Fray Antonio de Jesús threatens from Baeza that he will not leave me here for long. Be that as it may, for in the meanwhile I am well off without knowing anything, and the life of the desert is admirable.
>
> This morning we have already returned from gathering chick peas, and so the mornings go by. On another day we

shall thresh them. It is nice to handle these mute creatures, better than being badly handled by living ones. God grant that I may stay here. Pray for this, my daughter. But even though I am so happy here, I would not fail to come should you desire.

Take care of your soul. . . . Look after your health and do not fail to pray when you can.[3]

La Peñuela suited him. He was now far from the bickering and the maneuvering of the Consulta and various factions of the order. There is no doubt that he had been hurt by his rejection at the General Chapter. He relished this time of quiet and solitude for recovery from the hurt (and perhaps even bitterness) that is revealed in his letter.

He was soon to discover, however, that something was going on behind his back. One of the Definitors elected in the Madrid Chapter had been given the task of going to two or three monasteries in Andalusia to investigate the former provincial, Padre Gracian. To accomplish this assignment thoroughly, he was given the title of Visitor General with rather sweeping powers and authority. However, he did not confine himself to the case of Gracian. Rather, he also attempted to discredit Fray Juan. He asked questions in an awkward fashion and even scandalized some of the nuns by the suggestions implicit in his questions. He attempted to impute evil actions to Fray Juan, and when the sisters did not answer the way he wanted, he would interpret their responses. He was not even beyond changing some of the things they had said. Some members of the community hated Fray Juan and they believed the stories the Visitor was perpetrating. Others were indifferent. Those who were devoted to him were horrified and told Fray Juan, who was deeply hurt. Even La Peñuela could not harbor him from the pain of being attacked unjustly. Yet even now he refused to allow anyone to speak harshly about the man who was doing this. He maintained this attitude even during his intense illness. Without encountering any really strong opposition to his methods, Padre Diego Evangelista continued his attempts to have Fray Juan thrown out of the order. Later when he heard of Fray Juan's death, Padre Diego expressed regret that death had taken him before he could accomplish his goal of expulsion.

By the beginning of September, 1591, Fray Juan's condition was getting worse. His right leg was inflamed and very painful, and a fever was developing. Finally, it was clear he had to get some medical help. On September 21, 1591, he wrote again to Doña Ana de Mercado y Peñalosa:

> I received here in La Peñuela the packet of letters the servant brought me. I greatly appreciate your concern. Tomorrow I am going to Ubeda for the cure of a slight bout of fever. Since it has been returning each day now for more than a week and does not leave me, it seems I shall need the help of medicine. Yet I plan to return here immediately, for I am indeed very happy in this holy solitude.[4]

He had been given a choice of going either to Ubeda or Baeza. Many had encouraged him to go to Baeza since he was well known there and they had better medical facilities. However, Fray Juan simply wanted to rest, and knowing he would have all kinds of visitors if he went to Baeza, he chose to go to Ubeda. He did this despite the fact that he knew that Ubeda was a relatively new monastery with few resources and that the prior, Padre Francisco Crisostomo, did not like him. When the prior had been a member of the community of which Fray Juan was the superior, Juan had reprimanded him, and Padre Francisco never forgot this. Now he was about to have his revenge.

The trip was not extremely long, but Fray Juan's condition made it seem like ages. The paths were rough. The roads were dusty. The autumn sun beat down upon the sick monk and his companion. Fray Juan had not been able to eat for some time now. His leg pained him more than ever. He felt feverish and nauseated most of the time. When the narrow, winding streets of Ubeda were in sight, Fray Juan was delighted. The yellowish-brown buildings lined the cobblestone streets. It was a relief for Fray Juan to know he could soon rest in a cell of the monastery. Upon his arrival, the monks greeted him very warmly, especially Fray Alonso de la Madre de Dios, who had been a novice under Fray Juan in Granada. However, the prior was not so welcoming. His monastery was having financial difficulties as it was, and he saw Fray Juan's arrival as just another problem. He made that clear to the sick monk who had come for a cure.

The room which was to be the final living place of Fray Juan on this earth was entered through a very low doorway. He did not have to lower his head because he was so short, but any average-sized person would have to bend down to peer into the tiny cell which barely had space for its single piece of furniture, a rough wooden bed. The ceiling was so low it gave one the impression of being in a poorly constructed box. As fall faded into winter, the cold winds blew right through this room; cracks and drafts were everywhere. But for now, it was a place to rest, and Fray Juan was grateful for it.

The day after his arrival Fray Juan de la Cruz was up and attending all the functions of the community. Though still ill and tired, he went to prayer, meals, and recreation with the others. The prior had ordered him to do so. He was not to receive any special treatment. When his illness forced him to remain in bed rather than go to the refectory, he was summoned by the prior and rebuked for his disobedience. A few days later, however, his sickness got worse and it became clear that he had erysipelas. What had begun as a very small boil now broke out into a series of very painful sores. The doctor was called.

When Dr. Ambrosio de Villarreal arrived at the tiny cell and saw the patient, he knew what must be done. It was necessary to scrape and cut the infected areas and remove the diseased flesh. No anesthetic was available. When he cut and took out the flesh, the pain was incredible. Yet, Fray Juan uttered not a sound. As the days went on, his condition got worse. His flesh was literally rotting even as he remained alive. Pus flowed constantly from his wound. Many bandages were used daily. The surgical cutting continued as well, but the patient did not improve.

Soon the news spread that a saint was dying in the monastery of the Discalced. Many people came to visit him from outside. Several sent special gifts to him or offered services to him. The monks of the monastery itself went to see him often. All of this annoyed the prior more and more. Finally, he refused to allow any of the monks to visit Fray Juan without his express permission. The prior himself went to see Fray Juan and did all he could to make him uncomfortable. During the visits he would tell him how imperfect he was and how he gave a bad example to the other religious of the house. The prior saw him as far too relaxed and loose in his religious behaviour and told him so. He was accused of seeking out too much comfort and even of rejoicing in his illness and all the attention he got as a result of it. The prior refused to get Fray Juan the proper food and medicine he required. If this was not enough, the infirmarian, Fray Bernardo de la Virgen, who slept in the same room with him to care for him, was ordered to cease being Fray Juan's nurse. This was too much for Fray Bernardo, who then wrote to the provincial, Fray Antonio de Jesús, to tell him what was happening. When the news of this cruel treatment reached him, Fray Antonio immediately went to Ubeda.

It was in the last days of November, 1591, that Fray Antonio arrived at the monastery in Ubeda. He reprimanded the prior severely and ordered that Fray Juan be given everything he needed and that if necessary he would pay for it all himself. Furthermore, he wanted to spend some time with his former companion of Duruelo. With other monks present, he began speaking about what they had suffered during the early days of the reform. Fray Juan became visibly impatient and reminded Fray Antonio that they had promised not to speak of those things. Though the provincial was silent for a while, the persistence of the monks who wanted to know all about it won the day. Little by little Fray Antonio revealed a great deal about those early days—much to the dismay of Fray Juan.

By this time the little monk's disease was spreading rapidly. He now had terribly deep and excruciatingly painful ulcers and tumors on his legs and back. He was wasting away; not much flesh was left on his tiny frame. One day they tried to move him, but he insisted on moving himself. They discovered the reason as he dragged himself along: a large tumor on his back caused him severe pain as they tried to lift him. Now they hung a rope from the ceiling over his head. By grabbing it and pulling himself up he could change positions from time to time. Just before his death, as he was pulling himself up, he said: "Thank God I am light."[5] He had not lost his sense of humor despite the pain he was experiencing.

The pain was more than physical. He had already heard of Fray Diego's attempts to have him thrown out of the order. A pouch of letters he had received that told him of what was happening hung at the head of his bed. Shortly before he died, Fray Juan ordered that this pouch and the letters it contained be burned before him. He wanted to leave nothing behind to cause problems for anyone after his death. Even as he was dying, he would not allow anyone to say anything about Fray Diego despite the dishonest things he was doing.

In all this, people tried to alleviate his pain and change his thoughts. One of the brothers suggested he get some musicians to come and play for Fray Juan. Interestingly enough, Fray Juan first agreed providing it was not too much trouble. The musicians arrived and began playing outside his window. It was now that Fray Juan reconsidered the plan. He called the monk back and asked him to pay the musicians and send them away with thanks. He was concerned that perhaps the music would distract him from a fuller attention to the "inner music" he was hearing. He knew he could still grow if he actually lived out the life he was given to have here and now. Sometimes he could do nothing else. One day when the provincial was speaking to him, Fray Juan said: "My dear Father, please excuse me if I cannot be attentive to what you are saying because my whole being is racked with pain." He could hardly pray. He could only live his final days hoping that he would not fail to be faithful. When the Provincial told him he would soon receive the reward he had suffered so much for, Fray Juan responded, "Do not tell me that, Father. Don't please. Tell me my sins." Then he remained silent with his eyes closed.

A week before he died, Dr. Villarreal saw that the end was near. He decided that it was time to inform Fray Juan. One of the brothers, though hesitating, said to Fray Juan: "The doctor has told us that the end is near." Upon realizing that he was dying, Fray Juan's face lit up. Finally after all this pain, it was soon to be over. Yet he lingered on for another week.

On Friday, December 13, 1591, Fray Juan knew instinctively that his death was close at hand. He asked to see the prior and begged forgiveness for all the difficulties he had caused him and the monks. The prior made excuses for not being able to offer him more because of the poverty of the house. The day was silent and cold. Occasionally, Fray Juan would ask what time it was. He seemed obsessed with the time. He would then close his eyes. At times the brothers thought he had died, but no, he was only being quiet. When he opened his eyes he would look at the crucifix at his bedside, kiss it and go back into silence once again. Around five in the afternoon, he again asked the time and requested the Sacrament of the Sick (Extreme Unction as it was then known). As the ceremony was conducted, he recited the prayers along with the other monks. Then he asked forgiveness of the friars for the bad example he had given them.

When the provincial insisted he speak some words to them all, Fray Juan de la Cruz urged them to always obey the rule and the superior, to love each other and to live in harmony. Then with profound tenderness he made the sign of the cross over them all. The rest of the evening he wanted to be alone. With just a few people around him, he prayed and kissed the crucifix. His pain was intense. At 11:30 p.m. he asked the time once more. Then he said: "The time is near, please call my brothers." Fourteen brothers came with candles, and as many as could do so crowded into the tiny room. The others remained in the hall just outside. The smell of burning candles filled the little space. The light flickered, casting shadows on the walls as they recited the *De Profundis*. Just before midnight, the dying man again asked the time. Some of the other monks then nervously looked for the prayers of departure. When Fray Juan heard the ruffling of pages, he looked at them and said; "Leave it for the love of God. Be quiet." A few minutes later when the prior began saying the prayers for the dying person, Fray Juan asked him to read instead some passages from the *Song of Songs*. As they were read, he kept repeating: "What marvelous pearls! What marvelous pearls . . . ."

The bell rang for Matins. Fray Juan asked, "What was that?" "The bell calling the brothers to Matins," they answered. "Glory to God. I shall say them in heaven," he replied, looking at each one as if giving them a personal message. Once more he kissed the cross, closed his eyes and said, *"In manus tuas Domine commendo spiritum meum."*[6]

Moments after midnight on the 14th of December, 1591, Fray Juan de la Cruz, the orderly of Las Bubas, the first friar of the reform, the prisoner of Toledo, the First Definitor, the lover of Jesus, died. His death was as his life: gentle, tender, and loving.

The night was finished. The search for nothing was over. He remained the one rooted in creation, the creation his God and he loved so much.

NOTES

1. *Living Flame of Love-B*, IV, 5. BAC, p. 919 (Kav., p. 645).
2. This painting still exists and can be seen in the monastery in Segovia where one also finds the tomb of Fray Juan de la Cruz.
3. *Letter* no. 26, BAC, pp. 992–993, (Kav. no. 28, p. 704).
4. *Letter* no. 28, BAC, pp. 993–994, (Kav. no. 30, p. 705).
5. BMC vol. 14, p. 399; BNM Ms. 19404, ca. fol. 176.
6. BNM Ms. 12738, fol. 355.

Epilogue

One would have thought that the death of this friar would have ended the drama and mystery that had marked his life, but this was not the case. As soon as he was dead, his emaciated body was gently cleansed, clothed in his old habit and prepared for the visits of those who would come from Ubeda and the surrounding areas to pay their final respects to the man they had loved. The slight smile on his face, the same smile that had gently encouraged so many in their own trials and proved an enigma to others who were less open to see the transcendent God who broke into this world in and through the life of Fray Juan de la Cruz, suggested the peace in which he had died.

During his months of illness, when he was confined to his bed in the monastery of Ubeda, people began collecting various things that had touched him. The bandages which wrapped his wounds were especially important to those who wanted to keep a memento of the man. Human beings are instinctively drawn to keep things that are connected with those whose lives have somehow captured the greatness to which human beings aspire. Though he was not a national hero, there had been something about him that had captivated the minds and hearts of many people, especially the nonpersons, the poor. He had been one of them and they knew it. The woman who had spent days washing and preparing those bandages in his last weeks knew it. The friar who had slept in his room during his illness knew it. The friars who were just beginning their religious lives at Ubeda at the time of his illness knew it. So, each in their own way tried to preserve what they could of his presence, a presence which they knew could be rendered concrete by pieces of bandages, of his habit, and even of his flesh. Such things became sacraments of his enduring presence. His fellow monks began taking pieces of his habit and other things that he had touched as they laid his body on the heavy wooden table that would itself henceforth have a new value because his body had rested on it.

Word had spread during his illness that this monastery housed a friar who was special. The doctor's surprise at the strength and patience of his charge could not be hidden. He would tell others of this little man's incredible approach to life and suffering and even death itself. "How could he be so utterly gentle and human in the face of such suffering and anguish?" The laundry woman had also heard of the one whose bandages she washed and she, too, spread the stories she had heard about him. The menial task of cleaning his wrappings gradually became more meaningful to her. It was a chance for her to soothe suffering and she put more and more of her heart into it. Along with the stories of his final days came occasional details of his life: he had been imprisoned and tortured by his own religious community; he had deeply loved his mother and brother despite what most people thought about "detachment" from such love; he had spent his life loving people who were in difficulty; he especially loved the poor, the uneducated. In short, his life had given even those who had never met him personally a strange sense that God, who had shown Himself in Jesus, was indeed a lover of humanity, especially of those whom society regards as unimportant. There were not many people in that town of Ubeda who had not heard of him by this chilly December 14.

Consequently, when the monastery bells rang around one in the morning of the fourteenth, groups of people began to gather. The people started to move through the narrow streets toward the monastery. In the chilling winter rain, with the wind blowing and whistling through the streets, the town on the hillside began to come alive with men and women coming toward the tolling sounds which beckoned them to see for themselves the one they had heard about so often in the past weeks. The poor, who constituted the majority of the inhabitants of Ubeda, walked shoulder to shoulder with the rich. They entered the monastery hall to see the friar's withered body laid on the table surrounded by thick wax candles. The smell of the burning wax filled the room as they kissed his feet and hands. While the monks of the Discalced watched and tried to prevent them from doing so, people tore off little pieces of his habit to take home with them.

By the following morning, those who had not heard the bell or not understood its meaning learned what had happened and joined the crowd at the monastery. The crowd was so dense that the religious of the monastery had difficulty in clearing a path so that they could take the body of Fray Juan de la Cruz to the chapel. The scene of the night before was repeated: people came in to kneel and to kiss Juan's feet and hands and they tried to get a memento to take home with them so that they would have something which would reconstitute the little friar's presence. A Dominican who had known Fray Juan actually planned to cut off one of the fingers from the frail body but was hindered from doing so. However, the crowd was so great that some people actually succeeded in obtaining not only part of the habit, but even small pieces of the body itself.

Gradually, order was established and the service for the dead commenced. During the whole of the Eucharist, both the lay people and clergy realized that this was not simply the funeral service of an ordinary monk, but of one who had shown how deeply God's love could be incarnated in a human being and how warmly it could go out compassionately

towards others. There were certainly some among those present who even now did not like the man, but they, too, saw
that the general feeling was one of admiration. Dr. Becerra,
his friend from the days he had lived in Baeza, preached the
homily, noting that this was not so much an occasion to seek
God's mercy as an opportunity to render thanks for the gift
that each of them had been given through the life of Fray
Juan de la Cruz. Here indeed was a saint, even if people did
not realize the full implications of that in Fray Juan. When
the Mass was finished and the prayers for the dead recited according to the ancient ritual, the people carried the body to
its grave, but the burial was not to be the end of the unfolding
drama.

Señora Ana de Peñalosa, who had been such a close friend
of Fray Juan and who had enabled him to establish the monastery of the Discalced in the city of Segovia several years earlier, believed that his body should rest there rather than in
Ubeda. So she asked Fray Nicolas de Jesús María to grant permission for the body to be taken from Ubeda to Segovia. Fray
Nicolas, the Vicar of the Discalced, acceded to the request and
gave letters that ordered the prior of Ubeda to give the body to
those who presented him with these letters. In 1592, some nine
months after the death of Fray Juan, Joan de Medina Baballos
went to Ubeda and presented the papers to the Prior. That
evening Baballos, along with two other men, the Prior, and
two religious, disinterred the body only to discover that it was
still intact, though certainly dried out. They had expected
that by now the body would have completely decomposed. So
rather than take the whole body, they cut off one finger to take
back to Señora Ana de Peñalosa and returned the corpse,
planning to remove it once it had decomposed.

Finally in 1593, thinking that the body had by now decomposed sufficiently to allow it to be transported, the benefactress and friend of Fray Juan once again sent the same person
to Ubeda to gather the remains. When he arrived in Ubeda

the same scene repeated itself. They presented the letters to the superior and around eleven at night the laymen and the religious went quietly to the grave to remove the body. But once again they found his body incorrupt. This time, however, they decided to take the body anyway and by midnight the small cortege unobtrusively left Ubeda for the north. The secrecy was important because they feared that if the townspeople discovered what was happening, a great scene of protest would erupt. To maintain the secrecy on their journey to Madrid, the body was placed in an inconspicuous box and they made their way through Baeza and other places often under the cover of night.

Before entering Madrid, Baballos sent word to Señora Ana de Peñalosa and her brother that they would be entering the city soon with the body. Preparations were made at the convent of the Discalced where, when the cortege approached, the doors were opened and in the presence of some of his closest friends and associates Fray Juan's body re-entered the monastery he had known several years earlier. While there they removed an arm for relics and put a new habit on Fray Juan's body. Then the cortege continued on its way to Segovia where he would be buried in the monastery in which he had felt so much at home.

Segovia received the body with the tumultuousness that had characterized the wake and funeral in Ubeda some two years earlier. After the arrival at the monastery, word passed quickly through the city that Fray Juan had finally returned and large crowds came down the hill from the city center to view the body and to pay their respects to this man whom few had actually seen while he still lived, but whom all had heard about. Rosaries and other religious objects were given to the monks who guarded the body so that they might touch them to the body before returning them to their owners who then honored them as relics.

When the citizens of Ubeda found out that the body of

Fray Juan de la Cruz had been taken from them, they were very upset. In order to get the body back, they knew that they would have to obtain special permission from a higher authority. So the leaders in the community sent special representatives to Rome to petition the pope to order that the body be removed from Segovia and sent back to its original burial place. Once in Rome, the leaders of this group so impressed him that Pope Clement VIII issued a Brief on October 15, 1596 seeking the return of the body to Ubeda. The body had been in Segovia for three years and everyone realized that should the body be taken back, serious tumult would arise. It seemed that things were at an impasse.

At this point the superiors of the Discalced Carmelites intervened and came up with a compromise that they hoped would settle the affair once and for all. They proposed that Ubeda and its monastery get the remaining arm and leg of the corpse (the monastery had already retained one leg) while the monastery of Segovia would retain the head and the torso. Despite all the difficulties that this solution might have entailed, it was finally agreed by all that this was the best answer and the dismemberment was performed.[1] Today in Segovia, high above a special altar built early in the twentieth century, one sees an ornate marble box that contains the remains of Fray Juan de la Cruz.

The Beatification and Canonization Processes

Twenty-three years after the death of Fray Juan de la Cruz the ordinary procedures to gather information for the beatification of the Friar began. From 1614 to 1616 the officials gathered material in Medina del Campo, Segovia, Avila, Jaen, Baeza, Ubeda, Alcaudete, and Malaga without the official intervention of Rome. Yet, it was another eleven years (1627) before the Apostolic Process which added Salamanca to its list and accepted the material gathered in the earlier process was held. In fact, the beatification did not take place until 1675 and the canonization itself came only in 1726. Many were surprised at the long delay because they had expected that the process would move as rapidly as it had for Teresa de Avila, who died in 1582 and was canonized in 1622. The question remains: "Why did it take so long?" Part of the answer lies in the conflicts between Ubeda and Segovia, in the ancient antipathy between Andalusia and Castile. Moreover, we know from Madre Ana de Jesús, the fervent disciple of Teresa and friend of Fray Juan, that some people who formed part of the leadership of the order still disliked Fray Juan years after his death. These people may not have been anxious to have him officially raised to the status of saint. There were certainly very serious political overtones that played a role in the delay.

Furthermore, the almost incredible love for relics caused some problems. We have already seen how strong the Spanish desire for relics and the miracles resulting from them was in the people of Ubeda and Segovia. In 1625 the Roman authorities adamantly opposed the public veneration of people without the previous approval of Rome. On the morning of October 30, 1647, the people of Segovia and the Carmelites of the Discalced monastery there were surprised to find two official documents nailed to the doors of the Carmelite Church. These documents noted that Rome had expressly forbidden the placing of the remains of persons having a reputation for sanctity in a prominent place. Furthermore, it stated that the body of Fray Juan de la Cruz was venerated in this church in such a way that it had contravened these regulations.[2]

The following day a letter from the General of the Order, Fray Juan Bautista, dated October 31, 1647, ordered Padre Fray Bartolomé de Santa María, who was residing in the monastery at Segovia, to see to it that the body of Fray Juan de la Cruz was removed from its place of honor and buried in the ground as was customary. Within four days, the deed was done and the bishop was notified of the fact. Soon thereafter an official of the diocese was sent to investigate and verify that the body had actually been removed from its former place and put in one which was in accord with the Roman decree. When the fact had been confirmed, the officials in Rome were notified in the hopes that the prompt obedience of the Discalced would avoid the complete breakdown of the process of beatification that seemed to be implied in the documents posted on the church doors. For the next year or so the Discalced tried to get the process for the beatification underway once more. Rome moved very slowly and it was necessary to go step by step until finally in 1649 they convinced the pontiff himself to intervene and push the process ahead. This had been accomplished only through the personal intervention of King Felipe IV of Spain. The political route had unblocked the path, and now the process began to go forward with surprising rapidity.

On February 21, 1650, a large group of well-known and trusted people who had been especially selected because of their credibility came to the Segovian monastery of the Discalced to view the place where Fray Juan's body had been placed. They wanted to determine whether a public cult was going on around his body. A document dated February 21 states that Fray Juan's resting place is under the floor of a small chapel to the right of the church as one is leaving it. The group further discovered no pictures of the reformer of Carmel and asked where they, as well as the candles and other things that had been part of the cult, might be. The monks told them that in accordance with the earlier Roman decree they had been removed and placed in a secret place in the monastery under lock and key. When the group asked to see the place, they were brought to an obscure and remote part of the monastery where investigators were able to confirm that all these things were indeed well out of sight. Despite this, months and months of further examination of witnesses was necessary. Finally on November 26, 1650, it was declared by the tribunal that there was no worship or special veneration of Fray Juan de la Cruz in the Carmelite church. The process with all its papers was sent to Rome on February 9, 1651.

However, one more sensitive issue remained to be resolved. This was the question of the doctrine found in the works of Fray Juan de la Cruz. Throughout the whole of the sixteenth century and into the early part of the seventeenth, the *alumbrados* movement was very strong. This spirituality went to such extremes in accenting the interior life that its followers very often regarded the liturgy and even the authority of the Church as mere externals. While Fray Juan himself placed an emphasis on inner prayer, meditation and contemplation, he did not share the radical response of the *alumbrados* to the externals in the liturgy and to the authority of the institutional Church. In fact, he urged individuals not to be taken up with thoughts of visions, ecstacies and the rest which often became THE signs of holiness for the *alumbrados*. Nonetheless, one of the last groups of radical *alumbrados* was discovered in southern Spain in the first quarter of the seventeenth century and Fray Juan's works and those of Teresa de Avila were found in their library. The fear of mysticism and the desire to guard orthodoxy was certainly extremely strong at this time and this discovery would not have helped Fray Juan's process of beatification. The officials felt it was necessary to have his works thoroughly examined. Despite statements in his works that he submits all he writes to the judgment of church officials, the strong mystical dimension of his writings made him suspect. With all this in mind, Rome appointed a mature, respected theologian to examine his works. In his final decision, he noted that what was contained in the works of Fray Juan was also to be found in the scriptures. Therefore, it would be impossible to fault this reformer of Carmel because of the totally evangelical tone and content of his work. This meant that when the report came out in August, 1655 not only were his writings not condemned but they were praised for the depth and clarity they achieved in discussing such complex topics.

It would seem that all the hurdles had been passed and the beatification could take place, but again this was not to be the case. It was brought to the attention of the Roman authorities (by whom, we do not know) that there was a picture of Fray Juan in the Carmelite church in Toledo that was being reproduced and sent from this church to several countries in Europe. Would this process of *non-cultu* be started once again? The question of the veneration which seemed to be present had to be cleared up before the beatification could take place. Eventually, the case was investigated and found to be true and, as in Segovia, the cult was stopped.

Nonetheless, another question about Fray Juan's possible holiness was raised and had to be settled. It was noted that while Fray Juan was in jail in the monastery in Toledo, he was accused of pure stubbornness, rebellion against the authorities of the other branch of his order, and total disobedience despite his vow. These accusations would seem to destroy his claim to "heroic" virtue. Once again we might ask who raised this objection and why. However, we do not know. We only know that it was raised and ultimately settled. It was concluded that his attitude at that time was not rebellious (as it at first might have seemed) because he was working under the assumption that he had obeyed a higher authority, that of the papal legate. Then the question of certain miracles and apparitions that took place after his death came up. It looked like the beatification would never take place. Each step uncovered yet another objection and another until finally, the pope was asked to intervene once more. Though he asked that the process continue to progress, the discussion about the beatification went on almost up to the day of the actual ceremony. Ultimately, through the joint efforts of the Calced

and Discalced Carmelite orders, all the obstacles were
cleared away and Fray Juan was beatified on January 25,
1675 and finally canonized a saint by Pope Benedict XIII on
December 27, 1726.

Politics had slowed down the process, but very wise
political moves, as well as convincing evidence, caused Fray
Juan to be recognized as the deeply human and saintly man
that he was.

Segovia and Ubeda Today

Today the two cities of Segovia and Ubeda, which figured
so prominently in the life and death of Fray Juan de la Cruz,
are centers where his spirit still lives. The ancient stone walls
and houses here bear the marks of his presence. Amid the
splendor of palaces and monuments to other times sit the two
monasteries where he lived, died, and was buried. Within
their walls are housed the things that remind the visitor of
this great Spanish mystic whose influence is intensifying in
this technological age which seems so radically different from
sixteenth-century Spain.

Segovia, a short drive of eighty-eight kilometers northwest
of the bustling city of Madrid, draws thousands of tourists
yearly who come to see the ancient Roman aqueduct, the
spire-topped Cathedral, and the palace of the Alcazar. Very
few among them realize as they look down the precipice from
the Alcazar into the gorge below—where the Eresma river
flows beneath the black poplars reaching skyward—that just
beyond them lies the Discalced Carmelite monastery. Their
eyes take in a pastoral scene of green rolling hills broken only
by three buildings: to the right is the expansive Monastery del
Parral, in the middle is the striking, though much smaller
Church of the Vera Cruz, while to the left one sees the Monastery de San Juan, a maze of inter-connected buildings with
the inner square cloister clearly visible. If time allows, the
visitor will go to see the Monastery del Parral and the Church

of the Vera Cruz to which all tourist leaflets draw attention, but he or she is not likely to go to the nondescript monastery in which Fray Juan lived. The visitor bypasses a remarkable place of beauty.

As one approaches the Carmelite monastery by walking down the steep hill and crossing the Eresma river, the silence that is broken only by the rushing sounds of the nearby river is in sharp contrast to the noise of the city now seen high above on the rocky cliffs. The monastery complex, built with weathered light-brown stone, is made up of the main church to the left and the monastery building to the right. The exterior is plain, but the marks of restoration finished in 1977 are evident.

Before 1975 the monastery that had housed as many as thirty monks and more in centuries past contained a handful of Carmelites in a run-down building. The inner cloister had been walled up and the garden it surrounded had been allowed to run wild. Heat and lighting were poor and dampness seeped through the extremely thick walls causing the paint to peel. A small cluttered room held some objects connected with the famous friar of the Discalced. The main church remained as it had been since the early 1930s when Fray Juan's body had been placed in an ornate monument in the side chapel. Through a back exit one could enter the monastery garden which rose rather steeply to the cliffs and caves where he had spent time in solitude. Tall grass and weeds grew, overrunning the occasional flowers which tried to push their way through the choking brush.

Today the monastery, still run by the Discalced, has changed. About 1975, after months of discussion with the historical monument preservation officials, the work of restoring and renovating the building began.[3] The results are a tribute to the devotion of the Discalced and the sense of beauty which inspired them. The walls that blocked the open cloisters were removed and a large sitting room covered with a giant skylight was built on the site of what used to be the cloistered garden. The original monastic cells along two sides of the cloister were restored and modernized to provide simple but comfortable places for monks and visitors to rest and reflect. Most of the larger rooms such as the chapter room were made into light and airy conference and meeting halls or retained as dining rooms. Objects connected with the life and times of Fray Juan de la Cruz were artistically placed throughout the monastery to create a harmonious ensemble of modern architecture and old *objets d'art*. Two examples of these art pieces are especially striking. A brick wall forms the background for the remains of an altar piece from the Carmel in Medina del Campo where Fray Juan had celebrated the Eucharist. Nearby, ensconced in a wall, is a beautiful white alabaster madonna lit from behind by a gentle light that illuminates its detail. Everything contributes to an atmosphere of simple beauty that enhances what is called The Center of St. John of the Cross, a retreat and renewal center for reflection, prayer, and growth in the spirit of the reformer of Carmel. The whole monastery complex has become a living monument to Fray Juan de la Cruz.

With a population of some 32,000 people, Ubeda today lies in the heart of Andalusia, about 320 kilometers south of Madrid. Not as famous as Segovia and off the beaten road between Madrid and Granada, fewer visitors come to see this remarkable town situated on a sloping hillside. Ubeda is a maze of narrow streets that suddenly open into plazas containing historical buildings such as the Palacio de las Cadenas and the Sacra Capilla del Salvador, among many others. If one walks southward down the narrow, sloping street called Mortiel past gray stone buildings of a much earlier time huddling right on the sidewalk, one enters the plaza dominated by the Church of San Pablo. If one continues a short distance east on the street of San Juan de la Cruz, one arrives at the Oratory of San Juan de la Cruz, an unpretentious structure built of the same gray stone that seems to have been the common material for the construction of buildings here in the seventeenth century.

Though the Oratory was built in 1627, some thirty-six years after the death of Fray Juan, it is connected to the original monastery founded by the Discalced there in 1587. The choir loft of the Oratory is in fact the room where Fray Juan died on December 14, 1591. One reaches the loft through a series of narrow corridors in the adjoining monastery. Passing through a low door, one enters the tiny room that contains the table on which his body lay for a few hours after his death. On this table is a reliquary containing the leg and hand of Fray Juan de la Cruz, given to Ubeda after his body was taken to Segovia. Looking down from the loft into the chapel one discovers a catafalque on which rests a life-sized statue of Fray Juan reclining in death in the main aisle of the chapel. This statue has been placed over the original burial place of the frail monk of the Reform. The Discalced Friars who still maintain the monastery and the Oratory have made a small museum dedicated to Fray Juan in renovated rooms of the old monastery.

Though the dark, somber halls and rooms of this monastery stand in stark contrast to the light and simple beauty of the Segovian one, the visitor nonetheless senses the spirit of the last days of Fray Juan. Leaving these dark halls to go outside and turning left walking down the street, one sees just behind the monastery those lonely plains stretching far below filled with groves of olive trees and somehow knows that here, too, part of Fray Juan still lives.

The Sanctity of Fray Juan de la Cruz

When Fray Juan wrote, "At the evening of life, you will be examined in love...,"[4] he gave his readers the key to unlock the mystery of sanctity for his time and for our own. Having immersed himself in the Scriptures, he saw the command to love as the fundamental, radical call which God makes to every human being. To love God is to love one's neighbor, one's fellow human beings. The asceticism which He demands is to be found within the very structure of incarnating that love. Isaiah eloquently expresses the Word of Yahweh in this regard when he says:

> They ask me for laws that are just, they long for God to draw near: "Why should we fast if you never see it, why do penance if you never notice?" Lo, you do business on your fast days, you oppress all your workmen; lo, you quarrel and squabble when you fast and strike the poor man with your fist. Fasting like yours today will never make your voice heard on high. Is that the sort of fast that pleases me, a truly penitential day for men? Hanging your head like a reed, lying down on sackcloth and ashes? Is that what you call fasting, a day acceptable to Yahweh? Is not this the sort of fast that pleases me—it is the Lord Yahweh who speaks—to break unjust fetters and undo the thongs of the yoke, to let the oppressed go free, and break every yoke, to share your bread with the hungry, and shelter the homeless poor, to clothe the man you see to be naked and not turn from you own kin? Then will your light shine like the dawn and your wound be quickly healed over. Your integrity will go before you and the glory of Yahweh behind you. Cry, and Yahweh will answer; call and he will say "I am here." If you do away with the yoke, the clenched fist, the wicked word, if you give your bread to the hungry, and relief to the oppressed, your light will rise in the darkness, and your shadows become like noon. Is. 58:3-11

It was precisely because Jesus did this that he shocked and scandalised the "saints" of his time. And in freeing the oppressed He established a charter of love for His disciples, a love and compassion in and through which God the Father reaches out to all, especially to the nonpersons, the ones who do not count in our society. Today our growing consciousness of the absolute need for us as disciples of Jesus to be with and

concerned concretely and effectively with the nonperson is
yet another sign of what it is to be today's saint. Fray Juan
himself, though living in another time and culture, is a model
of that holiness, that wholeness brought about by and in the
Spirit who teaches all things (Jn. 14:26).

There is no characteristic that better describes the life and
personality of Fray Juan de la Cruz than this love. He loved
the poor, those oppressed by material and spiritual needs.
Think of him nursing the sick in Las Bubas in Medina del
Campo. His patients there were those without money, the
outcasts of their society because of their illness and their poverty. And they held a very special place in his heart and in his
loving compassion. One need but remember those other
monks and lay people whom he personally ministered to during the famine in Granada and during the plague in Baeza.
Then there were the children of the poor who lived in the
huts surrounding his own in the encampment around the Encarnación in Avila. He taught them and loved them. He even
called his brother Francisco "the greatest treasure he had on
earth." He loved and showed his love for this man even
though the society of his time said he should rather hide him
away. He loved him with an "attachment" despite the conventions governing all social conduct in that Segovian period.
The expectations of society were of no interest to him because
his life was based upon the command of the master who had
become his companion and friend. In short, deep human
love was the foundation for all his inter-relationships of sensitivity and compassion.

Over his lifetime Fray Juan became like the burning log
which is continuously attacked by the fire of love who is the
Spirit—until finally the flame and the log become indistin-
guishable. That love was a love of God he encountered in all:
his mother and brother, friends like Madre Ana de Jesús and
Dr. Becerra of Baeza, as well as Dr. Villegas of Segovia. Saint
and sinner, high and low were all deeply, intimately loved by

Fray Juan for they were, like him, part of God's creation and objects of His love expressed and incarnated through Fray Juan.

Moreover, he loved the whole of creation. He had to love it because of God's love for it. Through God he loved it all, which meant he truly saw that it was good. The way of denial which Fray Juan teaches in his works is but a technique to free the lover in each human being. By learning to let go and to allow the world and fellow human beings to be who and what they truly are, a disciple frees himself to love — to the death. Those who have seen him and his way to No-Thing (Nada) as being aloof and despising the world have totally missed the significance of Fray Juan de la Cruz.

Fray Juan's extraordinary delight in creation was the source of his strength. His gentleness and compassion did not mean weakness and failure. Rather, these qualities that were grounded in love gave him the strength to be faithful to his commitments and to live every aspect of his day-to-day life fully. His experience of the jail in Toledo, the demands of his positions in the order, the removal from all authority in 1591, his suffering of the malicious inquest into his past, his sympathetic understanding of the Prior of Ubeda's harsh and cruel treatment of him, and his painful death did not destroy who he was. Rather, all these things, including the joys of his life, created HIS life. His holiness was not something he was born with nor was it a sudden infusion of grace that turned him around completely. Rather that holiness, that wholeness grew in all his life experiences, and the love of God reached others through him in the midst of these events.

By living life fully, Fray Juan de la Cruz challenged the evil of his society and built up the good. Creation was not something apart from him. He was no angel in disguise. He was fully human, living his life in this world — and this was the life of God because he was rooted in creation, God's creation. Because of this, he is SAN JUAN DE LA CRUZ.

NOTES

1. The narration of these events can be found in Alonso de la Madre de Dios, *Vida, Virtudes*, fol. 301-340 with further detail and hagiographical additions.

2. For further details and information, see also the fine article by Fr. Tomas de San Juan de la Cruz, "Culto al 'Siervo de Dios' Fray Juan de la Cruz. Historia de unos procesos olvidados" in *Ephemerides Carmeliticae* 4-5 (1950-1954): 13-69. This has been the primary source for my discussion of Fray Juan's beatification and canonization procedures.

3 .The renovation work uncovered some surprises which have yet to be fully explained. For example, in the entrance, after removing the flooring, they discovered a large star of David made from bones set into a floor of small rounded stones. Could the monastery which Ana de Peñalos obtained from another religious community have originally been the home of a Jewish family? A synagogue?

4. *Sayings of Light and Love*, BAC no. 59, p. 963 (Kav. no. 57, p. 672).

Selected Texts from the Works
of Fray Juan de la Cruz

The soul will be clothed in God, in a new understanding of God ... and in a new love of God in God—once the will is stripped of all the cravings and satisfactions of the old man. And God vests the soul with new knowledge when the other old ideas and images are cast aside. He causes all that is of the old man, the abilities of the natural being, to cease, and attires all the faculties with new supernatural abilities. As a result a man's activities, once human, now become divine.

The Ascent I, 5, 7 (Kav., p. 83).

Accordingly the moment prayer begins, the soul as one with a store of water, drinks peaceably, without the labor and the need of fetching the water through the channels of past considerations, forms, and figures. At the moment it recollects itself in the presence of God, it enters upon an act of general loving, peaceful and tranquil knowledge, drinking wisdom and love and delight.

The Ascent II, 14, 2 (Kav., p. 143).

Any person questioning God or desiring some vision or revelation would be guilty not only of foolish behavior but also of offending Him, by not fixing his eyes entirely upon Christ and by living with the desire for some other novelty. God could respond as follows: "If I have already told you all things in My Word, My Son, and if I have no other word, what answer or revelation can I now make that would surpass this? Fasten your eyes on Him alone, because in Him I have spoken and revealed all, and in Him you shall discover even more than you ask for and desire.... For He is My entire locution and response, vision and revelation which I have already spoken, answered, manifested, and revealed to you, by giving Him to you as a brother, companion, master, ransom, and reward...."

The Ascent II, 22, 5 (Kav., p. 180).

The pure, cautious, simple, and humble soul should resist and reject revelations and other visions with as much effort and care as it would extremely dangerous temptations, for in order to reach the union of love there is no need of desiring them, but rather of rejecting them. Solomon meant this when he exclaimed: "What need has a man to desire and seek what is above his natural capacity?" (Eccl. 7:1) This means that to be perfect there is no need to desire to receive goods in a way that is supernatural and beyond one's capacity.

The Ascent II, 27, 6 (Kav., p. 202).

He obtains more joy and recreation in creatures through the dispossession of them. He cannot rejoice in them if he beholds them with possessiveness, for this is a care which, like a bond, fastens the spirit to earth and does not allow it freedom of heart.

The Ascent III, 20, 2 (Kav., p. 247).

It should be known, then, that God nurtures and caresses the soul, after it has been resolutely converted to His service, like a loving mother who warms her child with the heat of her bosom, nurses it with good milk and tender food, and carries and caresses it in her arms. But as the child grows older, the mother withholds her caresses and hides her tender love; she rubs bitter aloes on her sweet breast and sets the child down from her arms, letting it walk on its own feet so that it may put aside the habits of childhood and grow accustomed to greater and more important things.

The Dark Night I, 1, 2 (Kav., p. 288).

For contemplation is nothing else than a secret and peaceful and loving inflow of God, which, if not hampered, fires the soul in the spirit of love. . . .

The Dark Night I, 10, 6 (Kav., p. 318).

Softened and humbled by aridities and hardships and by other temptations and trials in which God exercises the soul in the course of this night, a person becomes meek toward God and himself, and also toward his neighbor. As a result he will no longer become impatiently angry with himself and his faults, nor with his neighbor's, neither is he displeased or disrespectfully querulous with God for not making him perfect quickly.

The Dark Night I, 13, 7 (Kav., p. 326).

And this is characteristic of the spirit purged and annihilated of all particular knowledge and affection: not finding satisfaction in anything, nor understanding anything in particular, and remaining in its emptiness and darkness, it embraces all things with great preparedness.

The Dark Night II, 8, 5 (Kav., p. 345).

It remains to be said, then, that even though this happy night darkens the spirit, it does so only to impart light concerning all things; and even though it humbles a person and reveals his miseries, it does so only to exalt him; and even though it impoverishes and empties him of all possessions and natural affection, it does so only that he may reach out divinely to the enjoyment of all earthly and heavenly things, with a general freedom of spirit in them all.

The Dark Night II, 9, 1 (Kav., p. 346).

Since the desire in which she seeks Him is authentic and her love intense, she does not want to leave any possible means untried. The soul that truly loves God is not slothful in doing all she can to find the Son of God, her Beloved. Even after she has done everything, she is dissatisfied and thinks she has done nothing.

The Spiritual Canticle 3, 1 (Kav., p. 428).

Not only by looking at them did He communicate natural being and graces, as we said, but also with this image of His Son alone, He clothed them in beauty by imparting to them supernatural being. This He did when He became man and elevated human nature in the beauty of God and consequently all creatures, since in human nature He was united with them all. Accordingly, the Son of God proclaimed: "If I be lifted up from the earth, I will elevate all things to Me" (Jn. 12:32). And in this elevation of all things through the Incarnation of His Son and through the glory of His resurrection according to the flesh, the Father did not merely beautify creatures partially, but rather we can say, clothed them wholly in beauty and dignity.

The Spiritual Canticle 5, 4 (Kav., p. 435).

St. Paul teaches this doctrine to the Corinthians, saying: "We do not wish to be unclothed, but we desire to be clothed over, that that which is mortal may be absorbed in life" (2 Cor. 5:4). This is like saying: "We do not desire to be despoiled of the flesh but to be clothed over with glory."

The Spiritual Canticle 11, 9 (Kav., p. 451).

It should be known that love never reaches perfection until lovers are so alike that one is transfigued in the other.
The Spiritual Canticle 11, 11 (Kav., p. 452).

Love produces such likeness in this transformation of lovers that one can say each is the other and both are one. The reason is, that in the union and transformation of love each gives possession of self to the other, and each leaves and exchanges self for the other. Thus each one lives in the other and is the other, and both are one in the transformation of love.
The Spiritual Canticle 12, 7 (Kav., p. 455).

Mountains have heights and they are affluent, vast, beautiful, graceful, bright and fragrant. These mountains are what my Beloved is to me.... Lonely valleys are quiet, pleasant, cool, shady, and flowing with fresh waters; in the variety of their groves and in the sweet song of the birds, they afford abundant recreation and delight to the senses, and in their solitude and silence they refresh and give rest. These valleys are what my Beloved is to me.
The Spiritual Canticle 14–15, 6–7 (Kav., p. 464).

So creatures will be for the soul a harmonious symphony of sublime music surpassing all concerts and melodies of the world.... Accordingly, she says that her Beloved is silent music because in Him she knows and enjoys this symphony of spiritual music.
The Spiritual Canticle 14–15, 25 (Kav., p. 472).

In the same way the soul perceives in that tranquil wisdom that all creatures, higher and lower ones alike, according to what each in itself has received from God, raise their voice in testimony to what God is. She beholds that each in its own way, bearing God within itself according to its capacity, magnifies

God. And thus all these voices form one voice of music prais-
ing the grandeur, wisdom, and wonderful knowledge of God.
The Spiritual Canticle 14–15, 27 (Kav., p. 473).

Because God vitally transforms the soul into Himself, all
these faculties, appetites, and movements lose their natural
imperfection and are changed to divine.
The Spiritual Canticle 20–21, 4 (Kav., p. 489).

For after the soul has been for some time the betrothed of the
Son of God in gentle and complete love, God calls her and
places her in His flowering garden to consummate this most
joyful state of marriage with Him. The union wrought between the two natures and the communication of the divine
to the human in this state is such that even though neither
changes its being, both appear to be God.
The Spiritual Canticle 22, 4 (Kav., p. 497).

Wherefore, since the soul lives in this state a life as happy and
glorious as is God's, let each one consider here, if he can, how
pleasant her life is; just as God is incapable of feeling any
distaste neither does she feel any, for the delight of God's
glory is experienced and enjoyed in the substance of the soul
now transformed in Him.
The Spiritual Canticle 22, 5 (Kav., p. 498).

The acts of the will are united to this flame and ascend, carried away and absorbed in the flame of the Holy Spirit. . . .
Thus in this state the soul cannot make acts because the Holy
Spirit makes them all and moves it toward them. As a result all
the acts of the soul are divine, since the movement toward
these acts and their execution stems from God. Hence it seems
to a person that every time this flame shoots up, making him
love with delight and divine quality, it is giving him eternal
life, since it raises him up to the activity of God in God.
The Living Flame I, 4 (Kav., pp. 580–581).

... it makes the soul live in God spiritually and experience the life of God in the manner David mentions: "My heart and my flesh rejoiced in the living God" (Ps. 83:3). David did not refer to God as living because of a necessity to do so, for God is always living, but in order to manifest that the spirit and the senses, transformed in God, enjoy Him in a living way, which is to taste the living God—that is, God's life, eternal life.

The Living Flame I, 6 (Kav., p. 581).

Joyfully and festively it practices the arts and games of love, as though in the palace of its nuptials, as Ahasuerus did with Esther (Esther 2:17). God shows his graces there, manifests His riches and the glory of His grandeur that in this soul might be fulfilled what He asserted in Proverbs: "I was delighted every day, playing before Him all the time, playing in the world. And my delights were to be with the children of men." (Prv. 8:30-31), that is, by bestowing delights on them.

The Living Flame I, 8 (Kav., p. 582).

It is noteworthy, then, that love is the soul's inclination, strength, and power in making its way to God, for love unites it with God. The more degrees of love it has, the more deeply it enters into God and centers itself in Him.

The Living Flame I, 13 (Kav., p. 583).

... the Father of lights (Jas. 1:17), who is not closefisted but diffuses Himself abundantly, as the sun does its rays, without being a respecter of persons (Acts 10:34), wherever there is room—always showing Himself gladly along the highways and byways—does not hesitate or consider it of little import to find His delights with the children of men at a common table in the world.

The Living Flame I, 15 (Kav., pp. 584-585).

When He wills to touch somewhat vehemently, the soul's burning reaches such a high degree of love that it seems to surpass that of all the fires of the world; for He is an infinite fire of love. As a result, in this union, the soul calls the Holy Spirit a cautery. Since the heat of a cautery is more intense and violent and produces a more singular effect than do other fires, the soul calls the act of this union a cautery in comparison with the others, for it is the outcome of a fire so much more aflame than all the others. Because the soul in this case is entirely transformed by the divine flame, it not only feels a cautery, but has become a cautery of blazing fire.

The Living Flame II, 2 (Kav., p. 596).

The happy soul that by great fortune reaches this cautery knows all things, tastes all things, does all it wishes, and prospers; no one prevails before it and nothing touches it. This is the soul of which the Apostle speaks: "The spiritual man judges all things and he is judged by no one" (1 Cor. 2:15). And again: "The spirit searches out all things, unto the deep things of God" (1 Cor. 2:10). This is love's trait: to examine all the goods of the Beloved.

The Living Flame II, 4 (Kav., pp. 596–597).

Whether a soul is wounded by other wounds of miseries and sins or whether it is healthy, this cautery of love immediately effects a wound of love in the one it touches, and those wounds due to other causes become wounds of love.

The Living Flame II, 7 (Kav., p. 597).

The Holy Spirit produces it only for the sake of giving delight, and since His will to delight the soul is great, this wound will be great, for it will be extremely delightful.

The Living Flame II, 7 (Kav., p. 598).

The fire issuing from the substance and power of that living point, which contains the spiritual and substantial veins of the soul, is the measure of the soul's power and strength. The

soul feels its ardor strengthen and increase and its love become so refined in this ardor that seemingly there are seas of
loving fire within it, reaching to the heights and depths of the
earthly and heavenly spheres, imbuing all with love. It seems
to it that the entire universe is a sea of love in which it is en-
gulfed, for, conscious of the living point or center of love
within itself, it is unable to catch sight of the boundaries of
this love.

The Living Flame II, 9 (Kav., p. 599).

In this state of life so perfect, the soul always walks in festiv-
ity, inwardly and outwardly, and it frequently bears on its
spiritual tongue a new song of great jubilation in God, a song
always new, enfolded in a gladness and love arising from the
knowledge the soul has of its happy state.

The Living Flame II, 36 (Kav., p. 609).

The true lover is only content when he employs all that he is
in himself, is worth, has, and receives in the beloved, and the
greater all this is, the more satisfaction he receives in giving
it.

The Living Flame III, 1 (Kav., p. 610).

You (the soul) were made wonderfully joyful according to the
whole harmonious composite of your soul and even your
body, converted completely into a paradise divinely irri-
gated, that the psalmist's affirmation might also be fulfilled
in you: "the impetus of the river makes the city of God joyful"
(Ps. 45:5).

The Living Flame III, 7 (Kav., p. 613).

. . . the soul knows creatures through God and not God
through creatures.

The Living Flame IV, 5 (Kav., p. 645).

Yet God always acts in this way—as the soul is able to see—
moving, governing, bestowing being, power, graces and gifts
upon all creatures bearing them all in Himself by His power,
presence, and substance.
> *The Living Flame* IV, 7 (Kav., p. 645).

Well and good if all things change, Lord God, provided we
are rooted in You.
> *Sayings of Light and Love*, no. 30 (Kav., p. 669).

Going everywhere, my God, with You, everywhere things will
happen as I desire for You.
> *Sayings of Light and Love*, no. 50, (Kav., p. 671).

At the evening of life, you will be examined in love. Learn to
love as God desires to be loved and abandon your own ways of
acting.
> *Sayings of Light and Love*, no. 57 (Kav., p. 672).

The soul that walks in love neither rests nor grows tired.
> *Maxims and Counsels*, no. 18, (Kav., p. 675).

Anyone who does not love his neighbor abhors God.
> *Other Counsels*, no. 9, (Kav., p. 682).

Jesus be in your soul. A few days ago I wrote to you through
Padre Fray Juan in answer to your last letter, which, as was
your hope, I prized. I have answered you in that letter, since I
believe I have received all your letters. And I have felt your
grief, afflictions, and loneliness. These, in silence, ever tell
me so much that the pen cannot declare it.
> *Letter 10*. To Doña Juana de Pedraza in Granada.
> Segovia, January 28, 1589. (Kav., pp. 690-691.)

Jesus be in your soul and thanks to Him that He has enabled
me not to forget the poor, as you say, or be idle, as you say.

For it greatly vexes me to think you believe what you say; this would be very bad after so many kindnesses on your part when I least deserved them. That's all I need now is to forget you! Look, how could this be so in the case of one who is in my soul as you are?

Letter 19. To Doña Juana de Pedraza in Granada.
Segovia, October 12, 1589. (Kav., p. 699.)

My Beloved is the mountains,
And lonely wooded valleys,
Strange islands,
And resounding rivers,
The whistling of love stirring breezes,

The tranquil night
At the time of the rising dawn,
Silent music,
Sounding solitude,
The supper that refreshes, and deepens love.
The Spiritual Canticle-B, XIII–XIV, (Kav., p. 714.)

My son, I wish to give You
A bride who will love You.
Because of You she will deserve
To share our company,

And eat bread at Our table,
The same bread I eat,
That she may know the good
I have in such a Son;
And rejoice with Me
In Your grace and fullness.

I am very grateful, Father,
The Son answered;
I will show my brightness
To the bride You give Me.

So that by it she may see
How great My Father is,
And how I have received
My being from Your being.

I will hold her in My arms
And she will burn with Your love,
And with eternal delight
She will exalt Your goodness.
  Romance 3. On Creation, 1–5. (Kav., pp. 726–727).

Let it be done, then, said the Father,
For Your love has deserved it;
And by these words
The world was created.

A palace for the bride
Made with great wisdom
And divided into rooms,
One above, the other below.

The lower was furnished
With infinite variety,
While the higher was made beautiful
With marvelous jewels,

That the bride might know
The Bridegroom she had.
The orders of angels
Were placed in the higher,

But man was given
The lower place
For he was, in his being,
A lesser thing.

And though beings and places
Were divided in this way,
Yet all form one
Who is called the bride;

For love of the same Bridegroom
Made one bride of them.
Those higher ones possessed
The Bridegroom in gladness,

The lower in hope, founded
On the faith which He infused in them,
Telling them: that one day
He would exalt them,

And that He would lift them
Up from their lowness
So that no one
Could mock it anymore;

For He would make Himself
Wholly like them,
And He would come to them
And dwell with them;

And God would be man
And man would be God,
And He would talk with them
And eat and drink with them;

And He Himself would be
With them continually
Until the consummation
Of this world,

When, joined, they would rejoice
In eternal song;
For He was the Head
Of this bride of His

To Whom all the members
Of the just would be joined,
Who form the body of the bride.
He would take her

Tenderly in His arms
And there give her His love;
And when they were thus one,
He would lift her to the Father

Where God's very joy
Would be her joy.
For as the Father and the Son
And He who proceeds from them

Live in one another,
So it would be with the bride:
For, taken wholly into God,
She will live the life of God.

> *Romance 4. Creation* (Continued), 1-17,
> (Kav., pp. 727-728).

Now You see, Son, that Your bride
Was made in Your image,
And so far as she is like You
She will suit you well;

Yet she is different, in her flesh,
Which Your simple being does not have.
In perfect love
This law holds:

That the lover become
Like the one he loves;
For the greater their likeness
The greater their delight.

Surely Your bride's delight
Would greatly increase
Were she to see You like her,
In her own flesh.

My will is Yours,
The Son replied,
And my glory is
That Your will be Mine.

This is fitting, Father,
What You, the Most High, say;
For in this way
Your goodness will be the more seen,

Your great power will be seen
And Your justice and wisdom.
I will go and tell the world,
Spreading the word
Of Your beauty and sweetness
And of Your sovereignty.

I will go seek My bride
And take upon Myself
Her weariness and labors
In which she suffers so;

And that she may have life
I will die for her,
And lifting her out of that deep,
I will restore her to You.

> *Romance 7. The Incarnation*, 1–11,
> (Kav., pp. 730–731).

For Further Reading

I have listed below some of the biographies of Fray Juan de la Cruz that I consider to be useful to those desiring further reading on the subject.

Fray Alonso de la Madre de Dios. *Vida, virtudes y milagros del santo padre Fray Juan de la Cruz, maestro y padre de la Reforma de la Orden de los Descalzos de Nuestra Señora del Monte Carmelo.* Biblioteca Naciónal de Madrid, Ms. 13460.
   This manuscipt was never published even though it was written by one who had known Fray Juan de la Cruz personally and had been involved in gathering the material for the beatification process. Because of the personal involvement of the author this particular work contains some details arranged in an orderly fashion that are impossible to find elsewhere.

Jean Baruzi. *Saint Jean de la Croix et le problème de l'expérience mystique.* Paris: F. Alcan, 1924.
   This work on Fray Juan is not primarily concerned with his biography, but the biographical section cited above is a superb interpretation of the life of Fray Juan. One cannot study seriously the life or work of Fray Juan without consulting this classical text on him.

Gerald Brenan. *St. John of the Cross: His Life & Poetry* (with a translation of the poetry by Lynda Nicholson). Cambridge: Cambridge University Press, 1973.
   A short and interesting presentation of the life of Fray Juan, employing some of the more recent discoveries and leaving out some of the hagiographical material found in other authors.

Fr. Bruno de Jesús-Marie. *Saint Jean de la Croix.* Bruges: Les Etudes Carmelitaines, Chez Desclée de Brouwer, 1961 edition.
   The original 1929 edition is available in English translation: Benedict Zimmerman, ed. *St. John of the Cross.* London: Sheed and Ward, 1936.

   The work by Father Bruno de Jesús-Marie is very interesting but highly hagiographical.

H. Chandebois. *Portrait de saint Jean de la Croix. La flûte de roseau.* Paris: Grasset, 1947.

A good work which provides one with the Carmelite milieu in which Fray Juan lived, as well as the basic events in the life of this mystic.

Crisogono de Jesús. *Vida y obras completas de San Juan de la Cruz.* (Revised posthumously with critical notes by Matias del Nino Jesus and critical edition, notes and appendices by Lucinio del SS. Sacramento), 5th edition. Madrid: Biblioteca de autores cristianos, 1964.

Without a doubt this is one of the most complete works giving the life and context of Fray Juan de la Cruz. It is of exceptional value for the scholarly material which is employed constantly. However, the author made no judgment as to the historical value of the incidents which he weaves together from primary sources to form this life of Fray Juan. An English translation from the 1955 edition was done by Kathleen Pond: *The Life of St. John of the Cross.* London: Longmans, Green & Co, 1958.

Jeronimo de San José. *Historia del Venerable Padre Fray Juan de la Cruz Primer Descalzo carmelita, compañero y Coadjutor de Santa Teresa de Jesús en la Fundación de su Reforma.* Madrid, 1641.

One of the earliest biographies but filled with strong hagiographical characteristics. It is nonetheless an important source for biographical information.

José de Jesús María (Quiroga). *Historia de la vida y virtudes del Venerable P. Fray Juan de la Cruz Primer Religioso de la Reformacion de los descalzos de Nuestra Senora del Carmen con Declaracion de los Grados de la vita contemplativa por donde N.S. le levanto a una rara perfecion en estado de destierro. Y del singular don, que tuvo para ensenar la sabiduria divina que transforma las almas en Dios.* Brussels: Ivan de Meerbeeck, 1628.

This work is highly hagiographical and contains the usual material found in the other earlier biographies. It is especially interpretative of the life of Fray Juan within the context that José de Jesús María sees as being that of holiness. For this latter reason, it is extremely interesting to read.